Cheyenne Memories
of the Custer Fight

compiled and edited by
RICHARD G. HARDORFF

Introduction to the Bison Books Edition
by Robert Wooster

UNIVERSITY OF NEBRASKA PRESS
LINCOLN & LONDON

© 1995 by Richard G. Hardorff
Introduction © 1998 by the University of Nebraska Press
All rights reserved
Manufactured in the United States of America

⊚ The paper in this book meets the minimum requirements of American
National Standard for Information Sciences—Permanence of Paper for
Printed Library Materials, ANSI Z39.48-1984.

First Bison Books printing: 1998
Most recent printing indicated by the last digit below:
10   9   8   7   6   5   4   3   2   1

Library of Congress Cataloging-in-Publication Data
Cheyenne memories of the Custer fight / compiled and edited by Richard G.
Hardorff; introduction to the Bison Books ed. by Robert Wooster.
p.   cm.
Originally published: Spokane: Arthur H. Clark, 1995. (Frontier military
series; no. 18)
Includes bibliographical references and index.
ISBN 0-8032-7311-8 (pbk.: alk. paper)
1. Little Bighorn, Battle of the, Mont., 1876—Personal narratives.
2. Cheyenne Indians—Wars, 1976.   I. Hardorff, Richard G.
E83.876.C54   1998
973.8'2—dc21
98-9239   CIP

Reprinted from the original 1995 edition by the Arthur H. Clark Co.,
Spokane WA.

That which is good in this work is
dedicated to the memory of
WILLIS ROWLAND

Introduction

Robert Wooster

When I learned of a new book about the Battle of the Little Bighorn, I must admit that, until fairly recently, my reaction was ambivalent. With all that had been written about this well-plowed field, the skeptic in me wondered if any new interpretation could plausibly be offered. I especially remember thinking this in the wake of reading Robert M. Utley's *Cavalier in Buckskin: George Armstrong Custer and the Western Military Frontier* (Norman: University of Oklahoma Press, 1988). Written by the dean of frontier military historians, this engaging and persuasive volume, I assumed, would become the standard interpretive framework for historical discussion of that bloody Sunday afternoon in June 1876, when Lakota and Cheyenne Indians routed most of the Seventh Cavalry Regiment.

I still agree with Utley's basic conclusions. Rather than viewing the Battle of the Little Bighorn as an army defeat, he explained, the engagement is more appropriately seen as an Indian victory. Well led, well armed, eager to fight, and determined to protect their families against the immediate threat posed by the soldiers, the Lakota and Cheyenne warriors demonstrated tactical skills that had long impressed western contemporaries. Utley also argued that Custer's tactical decisions were sound. Fearing that discovery of his presence would lead the inhabitants of the nearby Indian villages to escape the army's clutches, Custer decided to attack in the afternoon of June 25 rather than wait to launch the customary dawn strike the following morning. To Utley, this decision, even in the face of an enemy of unknown size and strength, was appropriate, given the army's previous experiences against Plains tribes, which rarely remained together in large numbers and often avoided pitched battles.

Custer, concluded Utley, was the victim of bad luck rather than bad judgment. The inhabitants of this Lakota and Cheyenne encampment were spoiling for a fight, buoyed by their recent success just eight days earlier against George Crook at the Battle of the Rosebud. Though Custer was responsible for the rampant factionalism within the regiment, Utley insisted, he could not fairly be blamed for the poor leadership displayed that day by his two battalion commanders, Marcus A. Reno and Frederick W. Benteen. Had Reno pressed his own attack against the village more vigorously, or at least held a threatening position among the easily defensible timber west of the river, Custer's charge could reasonably have been expected to incite panic and carry the day, Utley contended. Likewise, Benteen's failure to move quickly deprived Custer of any chance he might have had to launch a decisive strike against the still-unsuspecting Indian camp.

If Utley was a little vague about the exact details of Custer's last hour, I assumed, this simply reflected the lack of available evidence. After all, no one with Custer survived. Soon, however, a very different book convinced me that my rush to judgment had been a mistake. John Gray, a physiology professor and medical doctor, published his *Custer's Last Campaign: Mitch Boyer and the Little Bighorn Reconsidered* (Lincoln: University of Nebraska Press, 1991) three years after Utley's biography of Custer. Having previously written an influential survey of the entire campaign, Gray now turned his considerable detective skills to the battle itself. Linking scattered and sometimes contradictory records into a "time-motion" study, Gray showed that the oral testimony given by Crow scout Curley, long viewed as of dubious value, was in fact an accurate record of Custer's actions until about 4:45 P.M., when Curley was persuaded to escape while he still could.

By restoring Curley's reputation, Gray resolved many of the mysteries still clouding that afternoon's fateful engagement. Shaken by news that Reno had retreated in disarray and that the enemy held a huge numerical advantage, Custer divided his force at Medicine Tail Coulee, east of the Indian encampment and the Little Bighorn River. He now had no intention of making a headlong charge directly across the river into the campsite against heavy odds; rather, a feint made there would divert enemy attention away from Reno. Meanwhile, troops remaining under Custer's direct command could cover the probe, await Benteen's expected reinforcements, and prepare for an unopposed crossing further upstream. Of course, the ferocity of the opposition soon unraveled

Custer's hasty plan. The engagement itself, Gray demonstrated, was rather brief—no longer than forty minutes.

Armed with Utley's style and Gray's meticulous accounting, I once again believed that I had a good grasp of what really happened along the Little Bighorn. Soon, however, I was again forced to reconsider this assessment. In 1983, a grass fire laid bare the grounds of the Custer battlefield. Alert to the possibilities presented by this apparent concern, quick-witted National Park Service officials called in archaeologists to investigate the newly open terrain. Preliminary findings were published in 1987 and 1989; not until Richard Allan Fox Jr. completed his *Archaeology, History, and Custer's Last Battle* (Norman: University of Oklahoma Press, 1994), did I recognize the potential value of this approach. A trained archaeologist, Fox pointed out how the locations of shells discovered in the exhaustive fieldwork combined with a sensitive reading of Indian accounts to demonstrate just how disorganized Custer's battalion became in the brief engagement.

Fox's work, though often overstated, difficult to read, and too eager to demolish theories long dismissed by serious historians, nonetheless represented a signal contribution to Little Bighorn scholarship. I had now come full circle. Rather than feeling confident about my understanding of the battle and skeptical of "new" theories of the fate of Custer's men, I realized that there remains much work to be done.

Cheyenne Memories of the Custer Fight, assembled and edited by Richard Hardorff, fits in comfortably with the work of Fox and Gray. Before compiling this book, Hardorff had already written five other books about the Little Bighorn and its contestants, with special attention usually accorded the Indians. Indeed, his discussion of the number of Indian deaths at the Little Bighorn convinced Utley to reduce his own estimate, set at a hundred in his Custer biography, to less than half this number in his later *The Lance and the Shield: The Life and Times of Sitting Bull* (New York: Henry Holt, 1993). The present book, which in its careful documentation and attention to detail is characteristic of Hardorff's work as a whole, was originally published in 1995 by the Arthur H. Clark Company, a long-respected source of Western Americana, as a companion volume to Hardorff's earlier *Lakota Recollections of the Custer Fight: New Sources of Indian-Military History* (published by Clark in 1993 and recently reissued by the University of Nebraska Press as a Bison Books paperback).

Cheyenne Memories of the Custer Fight remains the single most complete published record in existence of Cheyenne accounts of the Little Bighorn. It includes five important components: eight interviews by George Bird Grinnell, a noted naturalist highly respected by the Cheyennes; four interviews by Walter M. Camp, an unassuming railroad man and historian of the Indians; five interviews with Two Moons, a leading Cheyenne figure at the battle; four miscellaneous interviews that reveal Cheyenne oral traditions about the engagement; and finally Hardorff's introduction and illuminating editorial notes. These varied Indian sources, as those scientist Gray and archaeologist Fox employed to such good use, represent a treasure-trove of material for the Indian Wars buff.

Several themes emerge. The accounts reprinted in *Cheyenne Memories of the Custer Fight* support Utley's criticism of Reno, whose premature retreat allowed the Lakotas and Cheyennes to concentrate their full fury against Custer. They also reaffirm the conclusion that the tribes did not realize the army was so near and had not lured Custer into making an ill-fated attack. Finally, no evidence is found here for the claim that large numbers of soldiers committed suicide during the battle. Popularized by Thomas B. Marquis, this claim was based upon stories supposedly gleaned from Cheyenne sources, including Wooden Leg, Howling Woman (also known as Kate Big Head), and Tall Bull. Hardorff failed to secure permission to reprint the Wooden Leg and Howling Woman materials, but as the present volume indicates, neither the Camp nor the Grinnell interviews with Tall Bull bore any suggestion of suicide. The men slain in Deep Ravine were neither members of a preliminary line of skirmishers nor practitioners of mass suicide; instead, they had tried to muster a breakout after resistance atop Custer Hill had been overrun.

The record is more mixed regarding the battlefield conduct of the Seventh Cavalry. American Horse remembered Custer's battalion as fighting well, as did Soldier Wolf. Brave Wolf is quoted as recalling that he "never saw such brave men." Acts of courage displayed by individual soldiers also pepper the records found here. But others suggest that many army units lost their cohesion. Reno's men "seemed to be drunk," thought Soldier Wolf. Similarly, White Bull noted that many bluecoats "acted like men intoxicated or beside themselves, as they fired into the air without taking aim." And while Two Moons recalled finding little ammunition among the dead soldiers, Young Two Moons recounted that tribal tradition held just the opposite to be true, a strong indication that resistance had been feeble.

How do we reconcile these conflicts? In all probability, both extremes were true. Faced with superior Cheyenne and Lakota numbers, the cavalry's efforts to mount a defense were hampered by the broken terrain, which allowed individual warriors to infiltrate the army's ragged firing lines. Attempts to hold frightened horses failed, thus spreading the disorder. Pockets of soldiers fought well and courageously; others, however, broke and ran or became paralyzed by fear. Panic spread as the troops lost cohesion and scrambled back frantically toward higher ground. With discipline shattered, the more individualistic fighting styles of the Indians overwhelmed desperate efforts to mount a final defense.

Problems remain for anyone hoping to compile a synthesis from traditional army files, recent archaeological discoveries, and the once-neglected Indian oral histories. Numerous gaps remain in the army records; after all, everyone with Custer at the end died. The archaeological digs came only after bodies had been repeatedly moved and souvenir hunters had pocketed countless numbers of shell casings, buttons, and other artifacts. And the Indian accounts, though valuable when used with care, have their own special quirks. Cultural differences, translation difficulties, loss of memory, and intentional obfuscation remain evident. In 1898, for example, Two Moons apparently told Hamlin Garland that he found 388 dead enemy bodies after the battle; eleven years later, he informed Joseph K. Dixon that there had been 488. Should this entirely discount Two Moons's recollections?

Despite these pitfalls, this paperback reprint of Hardorff's work is an important contribution to a significant historical event. Readers and researchers will now enjoy easy access to the Cheyenne side of this oft-told story. Students can use the source documents to draw their own conclusions, aware of the recorded interviews' inherent limitations but now free to check the sources for themselves. Hardorff's own interpretations represent another valuable resource. His careful explanatory notes and documentation of the quick disintegration of effective army resistance will surely influence future assessments of this fateful afternoon's events.

Where does this leave scholarship about the Battle of the Little Bighorn? I hope I've learned my lesson. Once a dreary old field left bare of nutrients by those who simply tried to squeeze more out of the land, the Little Bighorn has been rejuvenated by the introduction of fresh fertilizers and techniques, in the form of rich new sources and information. Publications like *Cheyenne Memories of the Custer Fight* offer a superb opportunity for someone interested in crafting a new synthesis about the battle that appeals to a broad general readership. Hardorff, Gray, and Fox have made important contributions; it is now time for a more elegant stylist to incorporate the body of evidence they have assembled into a readable account of the Lakota and Cheyenne victory against Long Hair and the bluecoats.

Contents

Illustrations

Maps

Preface

It was said among the Cheyennes that the wolves had known of the danger. The four-legged ones had trailed the white-faced strangers with the loud voices all the way from the Elk River, and since the wolves understood their language, they had learned the intentions of the whites. The loud strangers were sneaking through the night and were now moving towards the Goat River to attack the prairie people camped along the banks. It was said that the wolves had raced ahead and, from the rimrocks overlooking the valley floor, they had howled their warnings of the impending danger. But not one of the two-legged beings below paid any attention to the howling, except an elderly blind Cheyenne named Old Brave Wolf who understood their language. Yet, when he told his people of the terrible danger about to confront them, they doubted the wisdom of his words and ridiculed his pleas to heed the warnings. The next day, June 25, 1876, the Indian encampment was attacked by the Seventh U.S. Cavalry, and the battle of the Little Bighorn became history.

No armed confrontation with American Indians has received as much attention as has the Custer Fight. Fought on a Sunday afternoon, it resulted in the complete destruction of Lt. Col. George A. Custer and five companies of cavalry by Sioux and Cheyenne Indians. Two days later, members of the Montana Column found the mutilated corpses clustered in four groups on the battlefield. The bodies of C and L troopers were found strewn along Calhoun Ridge. Half a mile north from here, I Company was annihilated en masse in a little valley. A short distance to the west, on Custer Hill, some forty men had fallen around Custer, while near the river, twenty-eight bodies were found on the bottom of a deep ravine.

How Custer's command perished cannot be determined with certainty because no member of it survived. From the placement of the strewn bodies and combat refuse, the movements of his two battalions can be roughly reconstructed. But the details of the action, and the factors which shaped them, are bound to remain forever a mystery. As a result, controversy rages about Custer's strategy; the movements of his troops; and the order in which his companies were defeated. Speculation continues about such questions as to whether any or all of Custer's five companies went to Medicine Tail Ford, or whether the entire command marched together over Nye-Cartwright Ridge to the battlefield. Was Last Stand Hill indeed the location of the "Last Stand," or does this distinction belong to the defenders of Calhoun Hill? Did the twenty-eight men found on the bottom of Deep Ravine die there while in skirmish order at the beginning of the fight, or were they fleeing from Custer Hill at the end of the battle? And did the doomed troopers resort to mass suicide? These are but a few of the questions which continue to baffle both the scholar and the historian.

Evidence upon which to base any conclusions is inadequate, and as a result, the entire matter is now clothed in such a mass of supposition and theory that it is nearly impossible to separate the meager facts from the mass of conjecture. There exists, of course, an abundance of information accumulated through diaries, letters, orders and newspapers, but all of these sources contain impressions by individuals who viewed the field *after* the battle. There is, however, an untapped source which has been generally misunderstood and disregarded by many scholars. These are the accounts by the Indian combatants who were the only true eyewitnesses to the Custer Battle.

Those who sought to learn the truth about the battle encountered problems with the Indian interviews. These problems were caused by the difference in the cultural background, a difference which was rarely suspected. In addition, testimony delivered from an Indian frame of reference risked serious distortion in the process.

As I explained in *Lakota Recollections* (Spokane, Washington, 1991), Indian testimony has been discounted because of its apparent conflict with the known facts and theories. Fear of reprisals may have accounted for some of these distortions, while a general misunderstanding of the Indian frame of mind contributed to the problem. In addition to these facts, their statements were subject to inevitable forgetfulness caused by the passage of time.

It should be kept in mind that statements given by Indian informants were given in a language which was alien to the interrogator. The employment of an interpreter was therefore imperative. Thus, the success of each interview was based on the combined efforts and skills of three individuals. The outcome of the interview, therefore, was subject to the informant's knowledge and reliability, the translator's degree of language proficiency, and the interrogator's objectivity.

Examination of the translated Indian accounts reveals in a number of cases that the interrogator had preconceived ideas of the battle. Ignoring the need for historical accuracy, the information was modified through an editing process which called for sensational results. Then, too, the efficiency of the interpreter had a great effect on the outcome. His efficiency was based on his ability to understand the cultural background of the Indian, and his proficiency to convey the finer nuances of one language to another. Since most interpreters were barely proficient in the use of the English language, one cannot help but wonder about the accuracy of their recorded translations.

This lack of accuracy came to expression in many of the Lakota accounts. However, this is true to a much lesser extent with the Cheyenne accounts published in this volume because we know, in most cases, the reliability and degree of craftsmanship of both the interrogator and his translator.

If the cultural background caused a misconception, then the character and disposition of the Indian offered an even greater obstacle. The pre-reservation Indians were members of warrior societies. Out of necessity they lived according to combat rules designed expressly to perpetuate qualities which made for better warriors. Among these qualities were highly aggressive behavior, strong independence of personal actions, insensitivity to those outside the defined band or tribe, well-developed egocentricities, and concepts of property limited only to those within the tribal society itself. Is it any wonder, then, that such behavior shocked the Caucasian from an agrarian society, with strong European and puritanical roots?

In warrior societies, where social position depended almost solely on individual warlike actions, highly aggressive behavior became an attention-getting device and a means of status improvement. Used in combination with cultural egocentricity and insensitivity to persons and property outside the band, aggressive behavior approached the heights of virtue in a warrior society. Generally, the more forceful such behavior became, the more attention and increased status the perpetrator received from the warrior society itself.

Social esteem among the warlike Cheyennes was measured by one's military achievements. As a rule, therefore, warfare was waged for the greater glorification of the combatants. Loosely adhering to a common objective, each warrior applied his combat skills as he saw best to further his own interest. Other than planning and coordinating, Indian leaders had very little control over the conduct of each participant.

The battle at the Little Bighorn provided the Cheyenne warriors with a wonderful opportunity to display their prowess. Moreover, their exhibitions took place in full view of their families and nearly the entire Lakota nation. When asked later to give their recollections, the Indians only recounted personal incidents which rarely presented an overall view of the battle. Their statements were based on a series of impressions which conveyed only that which they had personally observed. These statements often lacked any reference to time and place. The Indian male was interested in his combat performance only, and later related his feats during kill-talks, a socially accepted form of bragging about one's accomplishments.

The cultural differences of the Indian are brought to expression in his recollections. It comes as no surprise, therefore, that the Caucasian mind judged these statements as confused, contradictory, and often in contrast with the known reality. Because of these irreconcilable differences, some researchers selected only Indian statements which suited their theories, while others ignored them altogether. Notwithstanding the shortcomings, the Indian side of the story offers a challenging and potentially valuable source of knowledge which, fortunately, had received a measure of creditability through the research of a handful of scholars, among which is Richard A. Fox, Jr., author of *Archaeology, History and Custer's Last Battle.*

This compilation contains nearly all recorded Cheyenne accounts. Not included, however, are the accounts by Wooden Leg and Howling Woman, the latter better known as Kate Big Head. Since I was unable to obtain reproduction permission, I refer the reader to *Wooden Leg* (University of Nebraska Press: Lincoln, 1962), and *Custer on the Little Bighorn* (End-Kian Publishing: Lodi, CA, 1971), both authored by Dr. Thomas B. Marquis. The recollections of these two Northern Cheyennes stand in sharp contrast with the testimony presented in the present volume. Both informants allegedly told Marquis that the Custer Battle commenced near present Deep Ravine, and that one of Custer's five companies, thought to have been Troop E, was completely annihilated there—not by the Indians, but through mass suicide!

The suicide theory has been mostly discounted by the academic community. However, based on the publications by Marquis, some scholars concluded that the first Custer casualties occurred near Deep Ravine. One of these scholars was Charles Kuhlman who developed the South Line theory. Kuhlman deduced that actually two companies (C and E) had been deployed near Deep Ravine and that a number of troopers were forced into and killed on the ravine bottom when the hostilities commenced, the survivors withdrawing to Custer Hill.

In the present volume, a companion work to *Lakota Recollections,* nearly all informants make clear that the destruction described by Marquis and Kuhlman did not occur at the beginning of the fight, but rather at the end; that the troopers involved did not act as a cohesive combat unit, but that these were panic-stricken men who fled from Custer Ridge; and, lastly, that these men died on the bottom of Deep Ravine, their deaths confirmed to be homicides, thus refuting the suicide theory.

In fairness to Marquis, it should be stated that he obtained his information through the use of Indian sign language. Although it was said that he was proficient in its use, it should be pointed out that this media only allows the transmission of broad concepts, and neglects the finer nuances of a language. It is conceivable, therefore, that some errors occurred during the communication process. Consequently, the possibility exists that *Wooden Leg* contains some passages in which the details are attributable to Marquis and not to his informants. Be that as it may, it is beyond doubt that the contributions made by Marquis to our historical knowledge far outweighs these possible shortcomings.

This publication contains the recollections of thirteen Cheyenne warriors, one interpreter, and a native historian. Scholars may recognize the names of such distinct individuals as American Horse, Brave Wolf, White Bull, Soldier Wolf, Tall Bull, White Shield, Bull Hump, Little Hawk, White Bird, Young Little Wolf, Two Moons, Big Beaver, Young Two Moons, Willis Rowland, and John Stands in Timber. The interviews were conducted by such notables as George Bird Grinnell, Walter Mason Camp, and Stanley Vestal. The recollections thus obtained by these men address some of the most perplexing questions which have confronted students of the Custer Battle. It is hoped, therefore, that the publication of these interviews will promote and stimulate the study of Native American materials dealing with this controversial episode in American history.

Acknowledgments

The compilation of this volume was made possible through the assistance of the following individuals and institutions. They have earned my enduring gratitude. Michael Wagner, Curator, Southwest Museum Library, Los Angeles, for permission to publish the George B. Grinnell interviews, and for his gracious assistance in answering my many queries; Dennis Rowley, Curator, Harold B. Lee Library, Provo, Utah, for permission to publish the Walter M. Camp interviews, and also to Leda Farley, of the same institution, for her patience in answering my many inquiries; Virginia Lowell Mauck, Curator, Lilly Library, Bloomington, Indiana, for permission to publish the Walter M. Camp interviews; Wayne Wells, Smithville, Tennessee, who submitted to me the articles on Two Moons in the *Harness Gazette* and in the *Kansas State Historical Society Collections;* Emmett D. Chisum, Research Historian, University of Wyoming Heritage Center, for locating the clipping of the Throssel interview; Linda Weirather, Billings Public Library, for locating the Long Forehead (Willis Rowland) interview; Doug McChristian, Chief Historian, Custer Battlefield National Monument, for permission to publish the Big Beaver and John Stands in Timber interviews, and for his gracious assistance on so many occasions; Brad Koplowitz, Assistant Curator, University of Oklahoma Library, for permission to publish the Stanley Vestal interview with Young Two Moons; Kitty Deernose, Museum Curator, Custer Battlefield National Monument, for her thorough assistance in locating photographic material; and Kathleen Baxter, Curator, National Anthropological Archives, Smithsonian Institution, for photo research. I am especially indebted to my wife Renée, for her valuable assistance throughout this research project, and to Bo and Casey, who accepted my pre-occupation without complaints—well, who did so most of the time.

Genoa, Illinois   RICHARD G. HARDORFF
May 25, 1994

The Grinnell Interviews

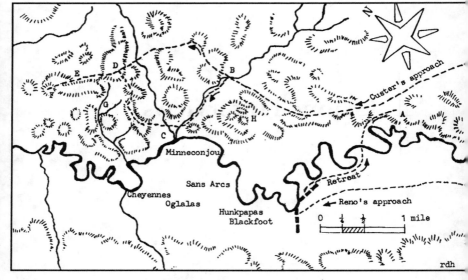

The Little Bighorn Battlefields, and Company Activity Locations

A) Reno Hill

B) Luce Ridge, from where E and F were sent to the river

C) Minneconjou Ford

D) Calhoun Hill, where members from C and L perished

E) Where I and surviving members of C and L perished

F) Custer Hill, site of the "Last Stand"

G) Deep Ravine, where 28 men were slain on the bottom

H) Weir Point, farthest advance of the Reno-Benteen force

George Bird Grinnell

George Bird Grinnell is best known for his publications on the North American Indians. However, his interest did not stop with that subject. Born in Brooklyn in 1849, Grinnell associated with the John Audubon family at an early age, instilling in him a profound interest in bird lore. As a result, he founded the Audubon Society which he financed and publicized by his own magazine, *Forest and Stream*. In addition, he was instrumental in the establishment of the Hispanic Society of America, and also the building of the headquarters of the American Geographic Society, the Numismatic Society, and the American Academy of Arts and Letters.

Grinnell was an ardent naturalist who campaigned to protect birds from commercial slaughter for hat decorations. He was a conservationist who fought for the resourceful management of all kinds of wildlife. In addition, he was a far-sighted man who accurately forecasted future droughts, dust storms and stream pollutions. He encouraged development of the National Parks as game preserves as well as places of natural beauty, and he served for many years as an official in the National Park Association.

Grinnell received a Ph.D. in zoology from Yale and was an

academic staff member from 1874 through 1880. During these years, he was the official naturalist on the Custer Expedition to the Black Hills in 1874, and the Ludlow Expedition to Yellowstone Park in 1875. From 1876 through 1880, he was the natural history editor of the Forest and Stream Publishing Company, after which he became its president, a position he held until 1911.

From 1892 until 1925, Grinnell contributed numerous scientific articles to many popular magazines, and at the same time he published a number of scholarly works on the Blackfeet, Pawnees, and the Cheyennes, all of which have become standard references. Known to the Cheyennes as Bird, their trust in him resulted in his intimate knowledge of their ways of life as evidenced in *The Fighting Cheyennes,* which is perhaps the finest publication in its field.

Upon Grinnell's death in 1938, his voluminous manuscripts, notes, photographs, clippings, and other data on Indians was measured to weigh nearly 500 pounds. This collection of historical and ethnological data was bequeathed to his friend, Dr. F.W. Hodge, and since the latter was then the director of the Southwest Museum, this research library became the repository of this truly impressive collection.

The following eight interviews were conducted by Grinnell during the years 1895 through 1908, and they are reproduced herein by special permission of the Southwest Museum. When possible, I have preceded each interview with a capsule biography of the Cheyenne informant.

The American Horse Interview

INTRODUCTION

Born in 1847, American Horse was a respected individual among the Northern Cheyennes. His leadership abilities resulted in his selection to the Cheyenne Chiefs Council, and he was later given the honor to place the stakes which mark the boundary lines of the Northern Cheyenne Reservation. He had one brother and two sons whose history went unrecorded. American Horse lived between Lame Deer and Birney, Montana, where a basin in the hills was named after him.

The original text of this interview, and the four which follow it, is contained in Grinnell's diary for 1895. However, due to the latter's handwriting style and the fading caused by the passing of time, the original penciled text is at times difficult to decipher. For that reason, I preferred using the typescript which was prepared by Grinnell himself. This typescript consists of three letter-size, double-spaced pages, identified as Item 497 of the George Bird Grinnell Collection. The following transcript is a verbatim copy of the original, except that I have corrected errors in spelling and grammar and have provided paragraphing and punctuation when lacking.

AMERICAN HORSE, A MEMBER OF THE CHEYENNE CHIEFS COUNCIL, IS
SEATED AT RIGHT NEXT TO TWO MOONS
Standing are Benjamin Beveridge and Interpreter Jules Seminole.
Photo by C.M. Bell taken during a visit of Northern Cheyenne
delegation to Washington, D.C. in 1888.
Photo courtesy of Smithsonian Institution, National Anthropological Archives.

THE AMERICAN HORSE INTERVIEW
Northern Cheyenne Indian Reservation, Montana, 1895

We first came together and heard that the white soldiers were in the country, down near the mouth of the Rosebud, close to the Yellowstone. A large camp gathered there. After a while, we all moved up the Rosebud, keeping scouts out all the time. While we were going up the Rosebud, we had a fight with the soldiers.[1] Afterward we crossed over to Reno Creek and camped. Scouts came in and said that lots of white men (soldiers) were coming.[2]

Next morning we moved on and camped in a big bottom where there is a bunch of timber, the place where we were afterwards attacked [by Custer]. Scouts were kept out all the time. The next day some men were back on the Rosebud, watching to see where the troops with whom they had fought were going. These went the other way, but these scouts discovered Custer going up the Rosebud.[3] A short time after the scout who made this discovery got into camp, four or five lodges of Sioux, who had set out to go to Red Cloud Agency, discovered Custer's troops close to them. These lodges got

---

[1]Reference is made to the Battle of Rosebud Creek, June 17, 1876, when Gen. George Crook's column was caught by surprise by a large force of Lakota and Cheyenne Indians. After a day-long battle, which resulted in surprisingly few casualties on either side, Crook withdrew to his supply camp to await reinforcements and thereby ceased to be of any further threat to the Indians. For a classic account of this affair, see J.W. Vaughn, *With Crook on the Rosebud* (Harrisburg, 1956); for a recent evaluation, see Neil C. Mangum, *Battle of the Rosebud* (El Segundo, 1987).

[2]This intelligence was probably brought by the prominent Brulé, Hollow Horn Bear, who, with a band of twenty Two Kettle Lakotas, observed Gen. Alfred A. Terry's Dakota Column near the Heart River during the latter part of May 1876. See Richard G. Hardorff, *Lakota Recollections of the Custer Fight* (Spokane, 1991), 178, and also the Throssel interview with Two Moons hereafter.

[3]According to the Minneconjou, White Bull, three Lakota scouts discovered Custer's column moving up the Rosebud on June 22. One of these scouts was Owns Bobtail Horse. See Hardorff, *Lakota Recollections*, 109.

frightened and turned back, and when they reached the main camp, their report caused great alarm.[4]

Above [on Reno Creek], where the Indians had left the Rosebud, two men, wounded in the first fight on the Rosebud, had died and [had] been left there in lodges. The troops discovered these lodges and charged them, and found not one there alive. The scouts of the Indians saw this.[5]

About this time, the troops turned and went to the head [of the lower forks] and there separated. The next thing I heard [was] an old man haranguing in the camp that the soldiers were about to charge the camp from both ends, the upper and the lower. I was in the Cheyenne camp, at the lower end of the village.

Then everyone who had a horse mounted it, but most of the men were on foot; they had no horses. Reno's party was the first to get down to the Indian camp, and most of the men went up there to meet him. I was with those who went to meet Reno, as he was charging down on the flat where the timber stands. When the troops reached this timber, they stopped and went into it, and stopped [again]. The Indians were all around them. Then the Sioux and the Cheyennes charged and the troops ran for the river. The Indians rode right up to them [and] knocked some off their horses as they were running, and some fell off in the river. It was like chasing buffalo—a grand chase.[6]

---

[4]The alarm was given by the Oglala, Black Bear, and six of his kinsmen who had spotted the smoke of Custer's bivouac fires along Davis Creek. See Kenneth Hammer, *Custer in '76* (Provo, 1976), 203. When interviewed in 1911, Black Bear was still afraid to admit his involvement due to fear of reprisals by the whites.

[5]The mode of burial identifies the deceased as Lakotas since the Northern Cheyennes preferred rimrock burials. It was said that one of these men was the brother of Chief Turning Bear. He had sustained a gunshot to his bowels and died in agony in his lodge on Reno Creek, on June 24. See Hammer, *Custer in '76*, 205, and also the Young Two Moons interview hereafter.

Reno's troops crossed the river and got up on the hill. Just as the troops got on the hill, the Indians saw a big pack train of mules coming, which met Reno there. The Indians all stopped at the river; they did not try to cross, but turned back to look over the dead for plunder, and to see who of their own people was killed.

While they were doing this, they heard shooting and calling down the river—a man calling out that the troops were attacking the lower end of the village. Then they all rushed down below and saw Custer coming down the hill and almost at the river. I was one of the first to meet the troops and the Indians and the soldiers reached the flat about the same time. When Custer saw them coming, he was down on the river bottom at the river's bank.[7] The troops fought in line of battle, and there they fought for some little time. Then the troops gave way and were driven up the hill. The troops fought on horseback all the way up the hill. They were on their horses as long as the horses lasted, but by this time the Indians had got all around them and they were completely surrounded.

Those [Indians] who were following behind picked up the guns and ammunition belts of the soldiers who had been killed, and [they] fought the troops with their own guns. Many of the belts picked up had no cartridges in them. The

---

[6]The retreat to the bluffs, called by Reno a "Charge," was a disastrous rout during which he incurred some thirty-five fatalities. Called by one of Reno's officers the *Sauve Qui Peut* Movement (Everybody for himself!), the Indians quickly closed in on the flanks of the stampeding troopers, ridiculing the panicky behavior of the whites with jeering calls. See John M. Carroll, *The Gibson-Edgerly Narratives* (Bryan, nd), 9, and Thomas B. Marquis, *Wooden Leg* (Lincoln, 1962), 221.

[7]Although some accounts deny Custer's presence at Medicine Tail Ford—and instead show his line of advance to Calhoun Ridge via Nye-Cartwright Ridge, a mile east of the river—the present witness makes very clear that Custer's force had reached the riverbank where the engagement started.

soldiers were shooting all the time, as fast as the Indians. There were so many Sioux and Cheyennes that the whole country seemed to be alive with them, closing in on the troops and shooting. They kept following them until they got to a high point, and by this time very few white men were left. Here they closed in on them, and in a moment all were killed. I think this ended about two or three o'clock.

After we had killed those on the hill, we discovered that there were some other white men who had gotten off. They were discovered by people down below, and were below, that is, downstream from the monument. They charged these and killed them all.[8]

After they had finished with Custer, they went back to Reno. It was now pretty late in the afternoon. They had fought there all night and all the next day until the middle of the afternoon. While they were fighting, someone came up the river and reported that troops were coming—a good many.[9] They left Reno and returned to camp, for they had made up their mind that they did not want to fight anymore. They had fought for two days now and thought that they had fought enough.

[Addendum by Grinnell:] Red Dog said to General [George] Crook—[Willis] Rowland being interpreter—that as nearly as he could get it, there were 1800 lodges in this camp, besides a great number of unattached young men from the agencies.[10]

---

[8]Two days after the battle, military survivors found the remains of twenty-eight men on the bottom of a washout, now known as Deep Ravine, some 700 yards southwest of Custer Hill. See Robert M. Utley, *The Reno Court of Inquiry: The Chicago Times Account* (Ft. Collins, 1972), 264.

[9]This force was Gen Terry's Montana Column which went into bivouac on June 26, near the present site of Crow Agency, Montana, some six miles north of Reno Hill. For a detailed account of the column's marches, see Edward J. McClernand, *With the Indian and the Buffalo in Montana, 1870-1878* (Glendale, 1969).

[10]This information was probably received by Crook in 1877, when he accepted the surrender of the hostile Lakotas at Camp Robinson in present northwestern Nebraska. Red Dog was a prominent Lakota leader of the *Oyukhpe* Band of Northern Oglalas. Crook's military career is chronicled in Martin F. Schmitt, *General George Crook: His Autobiography* (Norman, 1946). For biographical information on Willis Rowland, see the Long Forehead interview hereafter. For a study of the Indian population at the Little Bighorn, see the monograph in John S. Gray, *The Centennial Campaign: The Sioux War of 1876* (Ft. Collins, 1976), 346-357, and also Robert A. Marshall, "How Many Indians Were There?" *The Research Review* (June 1977): 3-12.

THE NORTHERN CHEYENNE, BRAVE WOLF, AND HIS WIFE CORN WOMAN
Photo taken by Laton A. Huffman on the Tongue River Indian Reservation in 1889.
Brave Wolf, who possessed the gift of prophecy, and who had been a Hohnúhk'e
(Contrary), was a man of much influence among the Cheyennes.
Photo courtesy of Custer Battlefield National Monument, National Park Service.

The Brave Wolf Interview

INTRODUCTION

Born about 1820, Brave Wolf was the son of Horn who was a famous prophet among the Northern Cheyennes. Brave Wolf was married to Corn Woman, the sister of Chief Crazy Head. However, Brave Wolf repeatedly treated his wife with disrespect, and it was rumored that he had an adulterous affair with Trail Woman, the sister of Two Moons, who was married to Long Jaw. Out of revenge, Long Jaw accosted Brave Wolf and cut off part of the latter's scalp lock. Being considered one of the outstanding fighters among the Northern Cheyennes, Brave Wolf's standing was not impaired by the scandalous affair. However, the disgrace was too much for his wife, Corn Woman, who left her husband. Later Brave Wolf gained revenge on Long Jaw who had committed incest with his own daughter, whereupon Brave Wolf drove him into exile.

Realizing how important Corn Woman had been to him, Brave Wolf beckoned her to return, which she steadfastly refused to do. In his sorrow, Brave Wolf then vowed to become a Contrary, and during the years from 1866 until 1876, he lived a solitary life of hardships. In combat he carried the contrary lance, also known as the thunder-bow, which possessed great spiritual power. While carrying this five-foot-long lance, Brave Wolf was always painted red, and he wore leggings, moccasins, and a blanket made from old, discarded lodge skins. His status as a Contrary did not allow him the comforts of a bed, and there were many other taboos associated with the life of a Contrary which made the rigors extremely hard to endure.

In addition to the spiritual powers of the thunder-bow, Brave Wolf also possessed the protective power of the swift hawk, which stuffed winged-being was worn on top of his head during combat. The protective power of this bird allowed him to charge close to the enemy while blowing a bone whistle and not be harmed. It was said that sometimes this bird would come alive during a charge and that it would whistle also when in close range with the enemy. This may have happened during the Rosebud Fight and the Custer Battle in which Brave Wolf played a prominent part.

In addition to the hawk, Brave Wolf also possessed an ancient scalp shirt which was handed down to him by his father, Horn. This shirt, too, had powers, which demanded that it was to be worn only by the very bravest. Brave Wolf later passed this shirt to his daughter's husband, Black Eagle, when the latter became a chief in 1864. This shirt was eventually purchased by George Grinnell who donated the sacred object to a museum.

Brave Wolf ceased to be a Contrary in 1876, when his thunder-bow was destroyed during the burning of Dull Knife's village. After the surrender of the Northern Cheyennes, he enlisted as a U.S. Indian Scout and fought with Gen. Nelson A. Miles against Lame Deer's band of Minneconjous and Chief Joseph's Nez Perces. The hardships endured as a Contrary, and his pitiful condition after Corn Woman left him, eventually resulted in his wife's forgiveness, and she returned to his lodge in the late 1870s. This time she stayed with him until his death in 1910.

The statement at the end of the introduction to the American Horse Interview regarding the transcription also applies to this interview. The typescript consists of a single letter-size, double-spaced page, identified as Item 497.

THE BRAVE WOLF INTERVIEW
Northern Cheyenne Indian Reservation, Montana, 1895

I was in the Cheyenne camp, and when Reno made his charge, I went with the rest to meet him. We fought there. I saw the soldiers all go down [into] the timber. I could never understand why they left it, for if they had stayed there, they would have been all right; but they ran out of the timber across the river and up the hill. The citizen packers and the pack mules were on the hill before Reno got there.[1] Then we heard the shooting below, and all rushed down the river.

When I got to the Cheyenne camp, the fighting had been going on for some time. The soldiers (Custer's) were right

---

[1] The pack train did not arrive on Reno Hill ahead of Reno. However, it may well be that Brave Wolf mistook the arrival of Benteen's battalion for that of the pack train. Lt. Luther R. Hare testified that he was dispatched from Reno Hill shortly after Benteen's arrival, to hurry the pack train and bring back two ammunition mules, an assignment which took some twenty minutes to complete. However, the pack train, which was plagued by numerous problems, was strung out over a long distance and reached Reno Hill nearly an hour after Reno's arrival. See William A. Graham, *Abstract of the Official Record of Proceedings of the Reno Court of Inquiry* (Harrisburg, 1954), 95, 96, 217.

[2] One of the most debated issues of the Custer Battle centers around the question of whether Custer actually attempted to cross the river. Was such an attempt made at Medicine Tail Ford *before* Custer was forced back to Calhoun Hill? Or was he never near the ford, but instead did his command travel straight from Cedar Coulee to Calhoun Hill? The early Cheyenne statements given to Grinnell suggest that Custer indeed reached the river and had quite a spirited engagement there. However, later Cheyenne accounts, notably of Wooden Leg and Kate Big Head, refute any combat at the river. Instead, these sources assert that Custer went directly to Calhoun Hill, and that his closest position to the stream was held by troopers at that location. The same contradiction holds true for the Lakota accounts, which are equally divided on this issue. However, modern field research now has established that soldiers were deployed near the ford and also on Luce Ridge, the heights situated along the north bank of Medicine Tail Coulee, about one mile east of the river. A reconstruction of the combat scenario suggests that the troops near the crossing were withdrawn onto Calhoun Hill before those on Luce Ridge followed. The latter movement was observed by the Indian reinforcements coming from the Reno fight, which might explain why these warriors denied seeing any combat action near the ford. Of course, we have to be careful with our conception of "at" or "near," which does not necessarily have to be at the river's edge. One of the few Indians who actually saw the two separate movements of Custer's troops was the Brulé, Two Eagles. See Hardorff, *Lakota Recollections*, 143.

down close to the stream, but none were on this side. Just as I got there, the soldiers began to retreat up the narrow gulch.[2] They were all drawn up in line of battle, shooting well and fighting hard, but there were so many people around them that they could not help being killed. They still held their line of battle and kept fighting and falling from their horses—fighting and falling all the way up, nearly to where the monument now stands. I think all their horses had been killed before they got quite to the top of the hill. None got there on horseback, and only a few on foot.[3]

A part of those who had reached the top of the hill went on over and tried to go to the stream. But they killed them all going down the hill before any of them got to the creek.[4] It was hard fighting, very hard all the time. I have been in many hard fights, but I never saw such brave men.

---

[3]The action described centers around the annihilation of the troops deployed on Calhoun Ridge, and the subsequent attempted withdrawal of Keogh's troop to Custer Hill.

[4]This is another reference to the men who were slain in Deep Ravine. Brave Wolf makes clear that these men attempted to escape from Custer Hill at the *end* of the fight.

The White Bull Interview

INTRODUCTION

The son of Black Moccasin, White Bull, also known as Ice Bear, was born about 1834, and he became one of the most respected shamans among the Northern Cheyennes. He acquired the healing powers of the bear, the antelope, and the wild hog, and he was instructed by the Thunder Beings in the making of several protective war bonnets, including the one worn by the celebrated warrior, Roman Nose.

White Bull married Wool Woman, who was the daughter of the prominent Cheyenne, Frog. This marriage resulted in the birth of his only son, Noisy Walking. Some evidence suggests that White Bull later adopted his nephew, Medicine Bird.

White Bull was already a prominent shaman in 1857, when the engagement with Col. E.V. Sumner's force took place on the Solomon Fork in Kansas. Although White Bull's shamanic power rendered the soldiers' guns harmless, irony had it that the troops charged into the Indians with sabres instead, against which the Cheyennes were not prepared.

A few days before the Custer Battle, White Bull officiated in the healing ceremony of a wounded Cheyenne. During this ceremony, White Bull heard spirits calling from the sacred mountain, Bear Butte, who informed him of the coming victory. White Bull fought in the Custer Battle and distinguished himself by grabbing

WHITE BULL, A PROMINENT SHAMAN AMONG
THE NORTHERN CHEYENNES
This photo by an unknown photographer was taken in 1897 on the
Tongue River Indian Reservation, Montana.
Photo courtesy of Smithsonian Institution, National Anthropological Archives.

a carbine from a soldier. However, the fight left a bitter memory
for White Bull because he lost his only son who was mortally
wounded.

After the surrender of the Cheyennes, White Bull enlisted as a
U.S. Indian Scout and served under Gen. Nelson A. Miles in the
campaigns against Lame Deer's Minneconjous and the Nez
Perces. It was said that White Bull's alertness had prevented the
killing of Gen. Miles during the opening phase of the Lame Deer
Fight. White Bull passed away about 1910.

The statement at the end of the introduction to the American
Horse Interview regarding the transcription also applies to this
interview. The typescript consists of a single letter-size, double-
spaced page, identified as Item 497.

THE WHITE BULL INTERVIEW
Northern Cheyenne Indian Reservation, Montana, 1895

Reno charged the camp from below and got in among the
lodges of Sitting Bull's camp, some of which he burned.[1] But
Reno got frightened and stopped, and the Indians caught
him and he retreated as [stated] in all the accounts. Then
word was brought that Custer was coming, and the Indians
all began to go back to fight Custer.

Custer rode down to the river bank and formed a line of
battle and [prepared] to charge.[2] But then he stopped and fell

---

[1]Reno did not charge into Sitting Bull's camp. According to Lt. George D. Wallace,
Reno's dismounted skirmish line was halted some seventy yards south of the nearest tepees.
However, Sgt. John M. Ryan and a detail of ten men may have advanced beyond the line.
According to Pvt. James Wilber, this detail reached the outskirts of the village, and it is
therefore conceivable that they may have burned some of the tepees. However, it seems
more likely that some of the lodges were accidentally set on fire by the terror-stricken
inhabitants in their mad rush to get away from the dangerous location. See Hammer, *Custer
in '76*, 148; Utley, *The Chicago Times Account*, 346; and John M. Ryan to Walter Camp,
11/29/1908, Walter Camp Collection, Brigham Young University.

[2]Like Grinnell's other informants, White Bull, too, recalled that elements of Custer's
command had advanced toward the village as close as the banks of the Little Bighorn.

back up the hill; but he met Indians coming from above and all sides, and again formed a line. It was here that they were killed.

From the men and from the horses of Reno's command, the Indians had obtained many guns and many cartridges which enabled them to fight Custer successfully. If it had not been for this, they could not have killed them so quickly. It was about eleven o'clock when they attacked Reno, and one o'clock when Custer's force had all been killed.[3] The men of Custer's force had not used many of their cartridges. Some had ten cartridges used from their belts and some twenty; but all their saddle pockets were full.

[Addendum by Grinnell:] From these accounts it would seem as though if Reno had charged through the village from below, and [if] Custer had kept on and charged the upper end, the two commands would have routed the Indians and got together. What they might have done, no one can tell. Owing to the panic of Reno's troops and their retreat, the Indians were enabled to destroy the two commands separately.

----

[3]Of interest is not the absolute time, but rather the opportunity it affords us to measure the lapsed time—two hours. However, according to the Oglala, Respects Nothing, the battle lasted three hours—from 1 p.m. until 4 p.m. He explained further that the readings came from a watch taken from one of Crook's slain soldiers. See Hardorff, *Lakota Recollections*, 32. For an analysis of the time confusion, see William A. Graham, *Abstract of the Official Record*, 37.

The Soldier Wolf Interview

INTRODUCTION

Very little information is available on this individual, and what meager references I was able to locate came from George Grinnell who knew him as a middle-aged and well informed man. Soldier Wolf was a Northern Cheyenne who was born in the 1850s. He was perhaps best known as the owner of a powerful protective charm which he wore in battle, tied to his chest, ever since his first combat experience at age thirteen. This charm was made of deer-skin and represented a naked human figure, its hair having been taken from the buffalo which gave it its protective power. In battle, this charm became the real Soldier Wolf, while the wearer could not be harmed unless the charm was hit.

The power of this charm was evidenced once again during the Custer Fight when Soldier Wolf charged at a soldier who tried to shoot him off his pony. Miraculously, the white man's carbine mis-fired and Soldier Wolf rode over him, knocking his adversary down. Turning his pony, Soldier Wolf charged at the soldier again, who by now had stumbled to his feet and who attempted to fire once more. But again the carbine failed to discharge, and Soldier Wolf then shot the white man in the chest. Let no one doubt the protective power of such a charm!

The original text of this interview is contained in Grinnell's diary for 1898. The comments regarding the transcription of the introduction to the American Horse interview apply to this document as well. The typescript consists of two letter-size, double-spaced pages, identified as Item 497.

THE SOLDIER WOLF INTERVIEW
Northern Cheyenne Indian Reservation, Montana, 1898

I was then seventeen years old, [and] old enough to notice a great many things and to see the reasons for it.

The Cheyennes had been there [on the Little Bighorn] only for one night.[1] Next morning, somewhere about noon, the troops charged down Reno Creek into the upper Sioux village, and drove all the people out and set fire to the lodges. When the people in the lower village heard the shooting up above, they all rushed toward it. Everybody went. The troops retreated and the Indians all rushed in among them. They were all mixed up. The soldiers seemed to be drunk (probably they were panic stricken); they could not shoot at all.[2] The soldiers retreated to the timber and fought behind cover. If they had remained in the timber, the Indians could not have killed them. But all at once—perhaps they got frightened—they rushed out and started to cross the creek. Then it was that the Indians rushed in among them. They crossed the river and went up the high bluff.

When the soldiers got on the ridge, the Indians left them.

---

[1]For the movements and the camp locations of the Indians prior to June 25, see the reconstruction by Gray in *Centennial Campaign*, 321-334.

[2]Although some alcohol was found among the spoils, statements of alcohol abuse and its devastating effect on the troops are without any concrete foundation, and are speculative at best. Most likely, the informant conveyed that the troopers *acted* as if drunk, which Grinnell rightfully construed as panic-stricken behavior. This agrees with the observation made by the Hunkpapa, Little Knife, who stated that Reno's retreating soldiers fired wildly over their shoulders, killing some of their own comrades, and that some of the troopers who became unhorsed confronted the Indians with arms raised in an appeal for pity. Of course, such foolish behavior was only ridiculed by the Lakotas and Cheyennes. See the partially-dated clipping of the *Billings Gazette*, 1926, Billings Clipping File, Billings Public Library.

When the Indians rushed to meet Reno, all the women and children gathered down at the lower village, and becoming more and more frightened as they listened to the firing, they decided to cross the river to the east side and so to get farther away from the fight. When these women were crossing the river and some were going up the hills, they discovered more troops coming. This was Custer's party.[3] The women ran back and someone rode to where the men were fighting Reno and told them that more soldiers were coming below. Then all the men rushed down the creek again to where the women were.

By this time, Custer had gotten down to the mouth of the dry creek and was on the level flat of the bottom. They began firing and for quite a time fought in the bottom, neither party giving back. There they killed quite a good many horses, and the ground was covered with the horses of the Cheyennes, the Sioux and the white men, and two soldiers were killed and left there.[4] But soon the Indians overpowered the soldiers and they began to give way, retreating slowly, face to the front.

They fell back up the hill until they had come nearly to where the monument now is. Then they turned and rushed over the top of the hill. From this point on, everything was

---

[3]While on the east side of the river, one of these women detected a squad of six troopers near Luce Ridge, this squad being well in advance of Custer's troops. See Walter Camp to Gen. Edward S. Godfrey, 5/28/1923, Francis R. Hagner Collection, New York Public Library; and also the statement by the Minneconjou, Standing Bear, who while on Black Butte, the Lakota name for Weir Point, saw the deployment of Reno's battalion on the valley floor and the sudden appearance of Custer's force on Reno Hill. See Raymond J. DeMallie, *The Sixth Grandfather: Black Elk's Teachings Given to John G. Neihardt* (Lincoln, 1984), 185.

[4]Although the slopes near Calhoun Hill were littered with dead horses, the flat on the east side near Medicine Tail Ford did not contain any such evidence. Capt. Benteen investigated this area for combat casualties, but he found the location void of any remains of either troopers or horses. See Graham, *Abstract of the Official Record*, 146. For a summary of evidence regarding casualties near the ford, see Edgar I. Stewart, *Custer's Luck* (Norman, 1955), 443-444.

mixed up, for there was a grand charge and nothing clear could be seen for the dust and the people, until all the troops had been killed. Then they ran off the government horses left alive, eighty or ninety head, down into the creek.[5]

After I had gone down with the horses and the fighting was over, the dust cleared away and I looked toward the hill—where the monument is— and saw many Indians still there. I went back to see what they were doing. As I went back, I found lying along the hill, north of the monument, a number of dead soldiers.[6] When I got on the hill, I found that all the soldiers had been killed.

In the fight, only six Cheyennes were killed; some were wounded but not very many. More Sioux were killed and wounded.[7]

Reno's men were frightened and acted as if they were drunk—as I think they were. Custer's men fought well and bravely.

---

[5]According to Trumpeter John Martin, less than half of the 210 horses of Custer's command were found slain on the battlefield. This observation agrees with that of Benteen who counted seventy dead horses. In addition to the cadavers on Custer's battlefield, the village site also contained a number of dead and wounded army horses, which makes Soldier Wolf's estimate of captured horses very credible. See Hammer, *Custer in '76*, 102, and also Graham, *Abstract of the Official Record*, 136. Not all the horses of Custer's command were lost. In addition to Comanche, a wounded grey horse of E Troop was also found on the village site. Named Nap, this shy little horse followed the troops to the Yellowstone and eventually reached Fort Lincoln where it was ridden for many years by the little children of the post. See Richard G. Hardorff, *Markers, Artifacts, and Indian Testimony: Preliminary Findings on the Custer Battle* (Short Hills, 1985), 66.

[6]Reference is made to the location where Capt. Myles Keogh's I Troop and survivors from C and L Troops were annihilated.

[7]The names of the six slain Cheyennes are Roman Nose, Limber Bones, Noisy Walking, Lame White Man, Whirlwind, and Black Bear. A seventh casualty, Cut Belly, succumbed to his wounds three weeks after the battle. See Richard G. Hardorff, *Hokahey! A Good Day to Die! The Indian Casualties of the Custer Fight* (Spokane, 1993).

The Tall Bull Interview

INTRODUCTION

Born about 1853, Tall Bull was the son of Stands All Night and Black Bird Woman, both Crow Indians who were captured at an early age by the Cheyennes. Tall Bull's brother-in-law was the respected Cheyenne, Lame White Man, who had married Tall Bull's sister, Twin Woman. Very little is known about Tall Bull, and the very few biographical references available were provided by John Stands in Timber, a maternal grandnephew.

Tall Bull was also an informant to Thomas Marquis who later stated that Tall Bull had witnessed the suicides of several Custer soldiers. After the surrender of the Cheyennes, Tall Bull served as a U.S. Indian Scout under Gen. Nelson A. Miles. In 1889, he enlisted in Lt. Edward W. Casey's troop of Cheyenne Indian Scouts and saw limited action at Pine Ridge during the Ghost Dance troubles.

According to a comment by Stands in Timber, Tall Bull must have been of amorous nature, he having "thrown away" at least five wives during Omaha Dances so as to be able to marry a younger one. Originating with the Omaha Indians, this dance was popular with the Cheyennes because of its spectacular nature and the general freedom it allowed from burdensome taboos.

The original text of this interview is also contained in Grinnell's diary for 1898, as was the previous interview. The comments on the typescript are the same as those made in the introduction to the American Horse interview. The typescript consists of a single letter-size, double-spaced page, identified as Item 497.

The Tall Bull Interview
Northern Cheyenne Indian Reservation, Montana, 1898

All the troops came down Reno Creek till they reached a small stream running from the north; there Custer left and went around to the east. Reno went on down to the Little Sheep Creek and crossed and charged into the upper Sioux village.[1] The people all ran out and the troops set the village on fire.[2]

All the lower-village people heard this and rushed up to where the soldiers were. Back of the village that was fired was a high hill, and the Indians all ran up on it and then charged down on the soldiers who retreated into the timber.[3] They did not stop there, but ran right through it and out on the other side.[4] I was present there and tried to cross the river. As

---

[1]When speaking of the Little Big Horn River, both the Cheyennes and the Crow Indians identified this stream by the mountain sheep which inhabit this region. The English rendition of this native name, therefore, should be written as "Little Bighorn." See Hammer, *Custer in '76*, 161, 212; and also the Walter Camp Manuscripts, Transcript, 824, Indiana University Library.

[2]In an attempt to drive any stragglers of Reno's battalion out of the woods, the Lakotas set fire to the grass near the Garryowen Bend. However, due to the moisture content of the vegetation, the fire failed to spread, but it did result in dense smoke, which may have been mistaken for the burning of the lodges. This smoke column was seen by the Montana Column which was then approaching the site of the present Crow Agency, the speculation being that Custer was burning the Indian village. See Utley, *The Chicago Times Account*, 96; Hardorff, *Lakota Recollections*, 103; and William Boyes, *Surgeon's Diary* (Rockville, 1974) 20.

[3]The vantage point spoken of is located southwest of Garryowen, on the south side of present Shoulder Blade Creek, near its mouth. See the account by the Lakota, Runs the Enemy, in Joseph K. Dixon, *The Vanishing Race* (New York, 1972), 172-173, and also Gen. Nelson A. Miles, *Personal Recollections* (New York, 1897), 286, who was shown this location by Lakota Indians in 1878.

the troops were crossing the river, the Indians kept killing them right along.

When the soldiers had all crossed the stream, news came to the Indians from down the creek that more soldiers were coming, and all turned back. They did not pursue the soldiers after they had crossed. All rushed back on the west side of the camp, down to a small dry run that comes in from the east, and there, down close to the river, were the soldiers.[5] The Indians all crossed and they fought there. For quite a long time the troops stood their ground right there. Then they began to back off, fighting all the time, for quite a distance, working up the hill, until they got pretty close to where the monument now is, and then the soldiers turned and rushed to the top of the hill. There they killed them all.

The horses—a good many—all ran down toward the stream northwest, and the people got about them and ran them off. A few soldiers started to run directly down toward Little Sheep Creek, but the Indians killed them all before they got there.[6] The horse I was riding had seven balls in him and dropped dead under me just before I got to the monument. Only six Cheyennes were killed in the fight, but a good many more Sioux [were slain].[7]

---

[4]Although the length of time is subject to speculation, Reno's battalion did halt in the woods, along which edge a second skirmish line was established. This location was hastily abandoned when a burst of volley fire fatally wounded Pvt. Henry Klotzbucher and Pvt. George Lorentz and instantly killed the Arickara, Bloody Knife. See Utley, *The Chicago Times Account*, 255-257.

[5]The dry watercourse spoken of is the present Medicine Tail Coulee, so named after the Crow Indian, Medicine Tail, whose land allotment is traversed by this coulee.

[6]This statement probably refers to the slain soldiers found in Deep Ravine. Note that these soldiers fled Custer Hill near the end of the battle.

[7]On June 25, the Lakota dead amounted to twenty-nine killed. On June 26, three more Lakotas were slain, while near the end of June two more died from the effects of their wounds. Thus, the Lakota dead count amounted to thirty-four people, among which were some ten women and children. See Hardorff, *Hokahey! A Good Day to Die!*

WHITE SHIELD, A SOUTHERN CHEYENNE, AT 25 YEARS OLD IN 1875
In this photo by John K. Hillers, the boy is believed to be
White Shield's eldest son, Porcupine, born in 1867, and known
to the whites as Harvey White Shield, who later graduated
from Haskell Indian College at Lawrence, Kansas.

The White Shield Interview

INTRODUCTION

Born about 1850, White Shield was known during his youth as Young Black Bird, son of Spotted Wolf and Wind Woman, and the paternal grandson of the renowned Cheyenne, Whistling Elk.

White Shield was a particularly brave individual and the owner of several protective charms. One was an ancient war bonnet which had been handed down by Whistling Elk. White Shield also possessed a stuffed kingfisher which was worn on top of the head during combat. The spiritual power of this bird protected not only the owner but also his pony, which had a kingfisher painted on its rump.

During the Rosebud Fight, White Shield distinguished himself through his brave feats. These included the killing of a Shoshone and several soldiers, among which was a noncommissioned officer; the counting of a number of coups; and the saving of Young Two Moons who was almost overtaken and killed by soldiers. White Shield died on May 2, 1918.

This interview was conducted at a much later date than the others, which might explain why Grinnell did not prepare a transcript. I have used, therefore, the original field notes, identified as Item 349, Field Notebook, 1908-1909, which consists of four pages of longhand, of which the following is a verbatim copy. I have corrected, however, errors of spelling and grammar, and have provided paragraphing and punctuation when lacking.

The White Shield Interview
Northern Cheyenne Indian Reservation, Montana, 1908

That morning I went fishing in the Little Bighorn with Black Stone and my nephew.[1] My nephew was catching grasshoppers for me. I know nothing about the Reno Fight. The boy sent after grasshoppers came back and said, "An Indian went by wearing a warbonnet—they must be looking for someone." I got on my horse and rode upon a hill and faintly heard much shooting and saw people running to the hills. I knew that the camp had been attacked. I rode into camp. What I had seen from a distance was the Reno Fight.

When I reached camp, all the men were gone, but my mother was leading my war horse around, down in front of the lodge, waiting for me. I bridled my horse and said to my mother, "Where is my war shirt?" She said that a man had just been here who took it to wear in the fight. His name was Bullet Proof. He fixed himself up to fight and tied a [stuffed] kingfisher to his head. (The same man who was in the Carpenter Fight.)[2]

While I was dressing myself and telling my mother which way she should go, I looked back and saw soldiers in seven groups (companies).[3] One company could be seen a long way off [because] the horses were pretty white.[4] I turned to go toward Custer, but some Indians had already seen Custer and were going toward him with others from the camps. I went around and came in below, though the company was coming fast, making for the Little Bighorn. Near me I could see only Roan Bear, Bobtail Horse and one other man.[5] On my side was a man named Mad Wolf who said, "No one should charge

---

[1]Black Stone was probably White Shield's half brother, while the nephew spoken of was probably the former's son.

[2]Known in his younger years as Wolf Man, this individual had taken part in the fight with Col. Nelson Cole on Powder River in 1865. During the engagement he was struck by two bullets, but miraculously neither projectile broke as much as his skin. Believing he was the owner of an unusually strong protective spirit, he changed his name to Bullet Proof and announced through the camp crier that henceforth he would serve the people as a shaman. By 1868, he had devised a powerful medicine which would render the soldier guns ineffective, allowing the Cheyennes to ride up close to the enemy and kill them without harm to themselves. Bullet Proof exhibited his powers during the Beecher Island Fight where he was pierced by a ball, but he closed the wound by rubbing it with his hand after touching the ground. One month later, the Cheyennes encountered Capt. L.H. Carpenter and a battalion of the Tenth Cavalry near Beaver River, Kansas. The attack was commenced by five young Cheyennes who wore animal sashes according to the instructions by Bullet Proof, and they had thus received the power to render the soldiers' bullets harmless. Unfortunately, the power failed and two of the young men were killed. Although Bullet Proof's standing as a shaman diminished somewhat in his band, he himself never lost any faith in his abilities. Perhaps it was for that reason that he borrowed White Shield's war shirt—not because of its protective powers, but because only a very few of the bravest men were allowed to possess such a shirt, and those who borrowed it were to show uncommon valor while wearing it. See George E. Hyde, *Life of George Bent* (Norman, 1967), 207, 309; and also George Bird Grinnell, *The Fighting Cheyennes* (Norman, 1956), 293-295.

[3]Custer's force consisted of five companies which were divided into two battalions, assigned as follows: Troops C, I, and L under command of Capt. Myles Keogh, the senior captain, while Troops E and F were commanded by Capt. George Yates, the whole force subject to Custer's command authority. See Hardorff, *Markers*, 24. The fact that White Shield counted seven soldier groups suggests that two of the five companies operated in platoon division.

[4]The white color of the cavalry horses identified this unit as Troop E. In the fall of 1868, the horses of the Seventh Cavalry were classified and arranged throughout the regiment according to color. In reference to Custer's force at the Little Bighorn, this arrangement had led to the following distribution: Troops F, I, and L had bay horses; Troop C had light sorrels, and Troop E had white or grey horses. Furthermore, the trumpeters rode greys; Adj. William W. Cooke rode a white horse; and as a rule, the officers rode horses of the same color as the company to which they had been assigned. See Gen. George A. Custer, *My Life on the Plains* (Lincoln, 1966), 269; and William A. Graham, *The Custer Myth* (Harrisburg, 1953), 346.

[5]Bobtail Horse was a member of the Elk Society and one of the first to oppose Custer's advance at the ford. After the surrender of the Cheyennes in 1877, he enlisted as a U.S. Indian Scout and saw service under Gen. Nelson A. Miles against the Nez Perces and Sitting Bull's Hunkpapa Lakotas. Bobtail Horse was a brave man, short of stature, and inclined to bashfulness when asked to tell his story of the Custer Battle. He had a brother named Hollow Wood. In the early 1860s his family was struck with tragedy when his sister committed suicide near Birney, Montana, the remains found hanging from a tree limb two years later. Roan Bear was a member of the Fox Society and, like Bobtail Bull, was one of the first to oppose Custer at Medicine Tail Ford. See Thomas B. Marquis, *Wooden Leg*, 98, 229-230.

yet—the soldiers are too many. Just keep shooting at them."[6]

When the Gray Horse Company got pretty close to the river, they dismounted, and all the soldiers back as far as I could see stopped and dismounted also.[7] When the Gray Horse Company dismounted, the Indians began to fire at them, and the soldiers returned the fire. It was not long before the Indians began to gather in large numbers where I was. After they had been shooting some time, Contrary Big Belly made a charge down in front of the Gray Horse Company[8] and from where the Indians were they saw that the horses of one other company began to get frightened and started to circle around the men who were holding them. When Contrary Big Belly got back, the companies began shooting fast.

---

[6]Born among the Southern Cheyennes in 1825, Mad Wolf was a member of the Dog Soldiers and is prominently mentioned during the tribal warfare with the Pawnees in the 1850s. In 1864, he was wounded on the South Platte during one of the frequent skirmishes which took place with the whites. He seemed to have had a liberal attitude toward his spiritual obligations. Failure to handle a medicine shield with reverence caused him to be wounded twice, while on another occasion he stalled his pledge to renew the Medicine Arrows, but was finally forced to complete the ceremony under pressure from the tribe. Mad Wolf died in 1905. See Grinnell, *The Fighting Cheyennes*, 85; Grinnell, *The Cheyenne Indians* (Lincoln, 1972), Vol.. I, 198, and Vol.. II, 195; and also Hyde, *Life of George Bent*, 122-123.

[7]Since E Troop was in the lead, it follows logically that the troops involved in this skirmish probably consisted of Companies E and F of Yates' battalion. For evidence regarding a division in Custer's battalion, see the statement by the Brulé, Two Eagles, and also Nicholas Ruleau, in Hardorff, *Lakota Recollections*, 41,143. For an analytical review of the two separate actions, see Jerome A. Greene, "Evidence and the Custer Enigma: A Reconstruction of Indian-Military History," in Kansas City Westerners *Trail Guide* (March-June, 1973): 14-24; and also Richard A. Fox, Jr., *Archaeology, History, and Custer's Last Battle* (Norman, 1993), 312-18.

[8]Grinnell identified this individual in *The Fighting Cheyennes* as Contrary Belly, but his field diary states the name as Contrary Big Belly. Very little is known of this individual, but White Shield's mention of him indicates that Contrary Belly's valor was not forgotten by his tribesmen. At the Rosebud, Contrary Belly had captured a pony from one of Crook's Indian scouts. This pony was given to Young Two Moons who was riding double with White Shield, both being hard pressed by pursuing members of Crook's force. This act by Contrary Big Belly may well have saved the lives of those two Cheyennes. See Grinnell, *The Fighting Cheyennes*, 335.

I looked across the river and saw two men make a charge on another company, far off to the southeast. These two men were Yellow Nose and my half brother.[9] It was here that Yellow Nose got a company flag, snatching it from the ground where it stood and counted coup with it on a soldier.[10] When Yellow Nose turned and went back towards the Indians, the horses of the frightened companies broke away from their holders and stampeded, causing someone to cry out, "The soldiers are coming!" The soldiers holding the horses did not let go; they hung on, but the horses got loose anyway.[11]

All the soldiers retreated back from the river; but the Gray Horse Company stood their ground. The Gray Horse Company stood [eventually] where the monument is now.[12] Of the other companies, some left the river, and some went toward it. The Indians charged from all sides and the compa-

---

[9]Born about 1854, Yellow Nose was a Ute Indian who was captured with his mother near the Rio Grande in 1858, by a Cheyenne war party under Lean Bear. This prominent Cheyenne adopted Yellow Nose as his son, and although he took the boy's mother as his wife, this woman twice attempted to escape and finally succeeded in 1860. Ironically, a few years after her return to the Utes, her daughter, a younger sister of Yellow Nose, was also captured by the Cheyennes. She later became the wife of Chief Spotted Wolf. Although short of stature, Yellow Nose grew up to become one of the most renowned warriors among the Cheyennes. At age 11, he received a severe gunshot wound in the chest during one of the many skirmishes with the whites in the Platte Valley in 1865. He survived his ordeal and joined the Dog Soldiers under Tall Bull. Although Yellow Nose was present during the destruction of Tall Bull's village at Summit Springs in 1869, he escaped the decimation of the Dog Soldiers and went north to join the Northern Cheyennes among whom he married. He was an active participant in the Rosebud Fight, but his accomplishments were overshadowed by the irreplaceable loss of an ancient buffalo shield. This shield, one which had protective powers, was the property of his brother-in-law, Spotted Wolf, who had lent it to him. Yellow Nose distinguished himself during the Custer Fight and earned several combat honors. After the surrender of the Cheyennes, he settled among the Southern Cheyennes in Oklahoma Territory. In later years he became a shaman. He was respected for his healing powers, and he led a pilgrimage to Bear Butte in 1909. He was still alive in 1915, a blind old man with many cherished memories of a life which no longer existed. See Hyde, *Life of George Bent*, 192, 297, 329, 335; Thomas B. Marquis, *Cheyennes and Sioux* (Stockton, 1973), 13; Grinnell, *By Cheyenne Campfires* (Lincoln, 1971), 69-71; Grinnell, *The Cheyenne Indians*, Vol.. II, 196.

[10]The interview does not make clear at which location the guidon was captured, and it is at this point in the narrative that students of the battle profess to have some difficulty understanding the sequence of events. Although the flag incident took place on the slopes of Calhoun Hill, White Shield failed to mention when the troops arrived here, or, for that matter, what had happened with the Gray Horse Troop seen at the ford. It is on such occasions that the Indian accounts appear to be bewildering, bringing into focus the cultural difference of the Indian frame of mind. However, when reading the interviews, one should be aware that the Indian recollections are basically a personal recounting of incidents, and that these incidents rarely present an overall view. Thus, the narrator's statements are based on a series of impressions which convey only that which had come under his personal observations. One should also keep in mind that these statements were nearly always self-serving, and that they more often than not lacked any reference to place and time. This, of course, was unacceptable to the Caucasian mind which dismissed these statements as being incomprehensible and often in stark contrast with the "facts" as the whites knew them.

In regards to White Shield's narrative, it mentions the gallantry of both Contrary Big Belly and, later, that of Yellow Nose, but it totally omits the withdrawal of E Troop from the river which took place before the assault on Calhoun Ridge commenced. Perhaps White Shield did not see this withdrawal or, more likely, did not think it important to mention as compared to the prowess exhibited by his two tribesmen. According to White Shield, Yellow Nose made his charge a long way from the river, "far off to the southeast." This seems to identify Calhoun Hill, which is corroborated by the map used by Willis Rowland in the Two Young Moons interview, which follows hereafter. It should be noted further that after capturing the company guidon, Yellow Nose seemed to have charged the soldiers on the hill a second time. However, this time he was not so lucky, he being singled out by the troopers as a target. A drawing by the Cheyenne, Spotted Wolf, shows Yellow Nose's pony being shot down under a hail of bullets while its rider still carried his lance and the captured company guidon. This incident was also noted by the Oglala, Eagle Elk, who remembered vividly that the Cheyenne was shot through the heels and that the pony stumbled, breaking both its legs. See Hyde, *Life of George Bent*, 192; Hardorff, *Lakota Recollections*, 104; and Peter J. Powell and Michael P. Malone, *Montana, Past and Present* (Los Angeles, 1976), 53-54.

[11]Each cavalry troop was divided into sets of four men and when ordered to dismount and fight on foot, the horses of each set were held by one trooper, freeing the other three to concentrate on combat activities. Considering the stresses caused by combat noise, it would have been virtually impossible for one man to control four horses by merely holding them by the reins. For that reason, the bridle was supplied with a strap on each side, along with a snap ring, which allowed the holder to link the bridles of the four horses together. See Daniel O. Magnussen, *Peter Thompson's Narrative of the Little Bighorn Campaign, 1876* (Glendale, 1974), 117. See also the statement by the Hunkpapa, Moving Robe Woman, who noted these horse holders near Calhoun Hill and saw them burdened with twice the number of horses normally allowed, which suggests a heightening crisis in which horse holders were deployed on the firing line. See Hardorff, *Lakota Recollections*, 95.

[12]This statement suffers from a sequential lapse which causes confusion in reference to E Troop, whose early withdrawal from Medicine Tail Ford is not mentioned.

nies came together a little.[13] By this time three companies (Smith, Crittenden and Calhoun) had lost their horses, but four still had theirs.[14] One company that lost their horses was near where the road goes now. They were all on foot, going toward the Gray Horse Company. I got around on that side. About half of this company was without guns. They fought with six shooters. It was close fighting, almost hand-to-hand, up that hill. The Gray Horse Company was on foot and kept the Indians off on one side and the other company came across in front of the Gray Horse Company.[15]

Three companies had been killed off before the second three companies and the Gray Horse Company were killed. The three still surviving were half a mile from the Gray Horse Company, toward the hill.[16] Those who survived from the first three companies tried to make their way to the Gray Horse Company, but they did not succeed as all were killed before they got there.[17] Finally, the three surviving companies

---

[13]These diverse military movements near Calhoun Hill were also noted by the Two Kettle Lakota, Runs the Enemy, in Dixon, *The Vanishing Race*, 176, and the Brulé, Two Eagles, in Hardorff, *Lakota Recollections*, 146.

[14]Grinnell's annotation has reference to Troop E, commanded by Lt. Algernon E. Smith, and Troop L, thought by Grinnell to have been deployed in two platoons, one commanded by Lt. James Calhoun, and the other by the subaltern, Lt. John J. Crittenden. Grinnell is in error about E Troop which kept their horses to the last.

[15]The road mentioned was actually a well-worn trail in 1908, which curved from Medicine Tail Ford onto Calhoun Hill, which it followed to the junction with Custer Ridge, and then curved north to Last Stand Hill. In 1934, a blacktop was laid to replace this dirt trail, which changed the definition of the ridge, among which was the gap used by Crazy Horse to charge across Custer Ridge. The action described by White Shield centers around the attempted military retreat from Calhoun Hill along the northeast side of Custer Ridge. For a similar description, see the observation of the Oglala, Foolish Elk, in Hammer, *Custer in '76*, 199, and also the account by the Minneconjou, White Bull, in Hardorff, *Lakota Recollections*, 113-115.

[16]The statement about "three companies killed off" refers to the troops deployed along Calhoun Ridge, which consisted of Troops C and L, of which one unit operated in platoon formation. See Hardorff, *Markers*, 45-46.

lost their horses and got up the hill on foot. After the three companies had reached the Gray Horse Company, a man riding a sorrel horse [escaped].[18]

The Gray Horse Company held their horses to the last, and almost all these horses were killed.[19] When the four companies got together, they did not last long. About when the last man dropped in the Gray Horse Company, the Indians made a charge and killed all the wounded with hatchets, arrows, knives etc. Old Bear and Kills in the Night, still living in 1915, chased the man on the sorrel horse, and Old Bear, I think, killed him. The Sioux fired a shot at this soldier but missed. Old Bear then fired, and a little later the soldier fell off his horse, and when they got to him they found he was shot in the back between the shoulders.[20]

---

[17]The survivors of Troops C and L fell back onto I Troop further down Custer Ridge, and only a few of these reached Custer Hill near which E Troop covered their retreat. See also the account by the Minneconjou, White Bull, who describes this very same action and confirms E Troop's position along Custer Ridge. See Hardorff, *Lakota Recollections*, 113.

[18]Nearly every Indian account contains a reference to the futile escape of a soldier, although these statements seem to describe different escape attempts. See, for example, the Young Two Moons interview hereafter, which describes a soldier fleeing toward Nye-Cartwright Ridge, while the Oglala, Flying Hawk, told Ricker that a soldier who galloped from Calhoun Hill to Custer Hill did not stop there, but instead kept going, to be killed about one-half mile further north. See Hardorff, *Lakota Recollections*, 52.

[19]Although these horses were nearly all killed near the end of the battle, not all were slain along Custer Ridge because military survivors found a number of dead greys near the head of Deep Ravine. This discovery later gave rise to the erroneous speculation that E Troop had been deployed at this latter location at the beginning of the Custer Battle. See the statement by the Hunkpapa, Iron Hawk, who saw the stampede of some of these grey horses near Custer Hill, while the Oglala, Black Elk, noticed a number of greys near the same location. See Hammer, *Custer in '76*, 191, 194. See also the statement by the Minneconjou, Feather Earring, who captured five greys who were wounded and trembling, but released them west of the river because of the severity of their wounds. One of these may have been the horse named Nap. See Graham, *The Custer Myth*, 97.

[20]Kills in the Night has not been identified. The man named Old Bear was probably the same individual who was known as a Cheyenne principle chief. Although a renowned civil leader, he nonetheless once violated the rules of the communal hunt, resulting in the killing of his horse as punishment by the camp police. See Marquis, *Wooden Leg*, 67, 205.

Custer was on the outer edge of the Gray Horse Company, toward the river. I saw the man supposed to be Custer being stripped. He was clad in a buckskin shirt—fringed on the breast—and trousers. He wore fine high boots, and had a knife stuck in a scabbard in his boot, and [wore] a big red handkerchief.[21] Lying near him was a six shooter and sabre. He must have died with the pistol in his hand. They had sabers with them.[22] A man supposed to be Custer had a long mustache, but no other hair on his face. He had marks pricked into his skin on the arms above the wrist. This was probably [Capt. Thomas W.] Custer.[23] The Indians did not charge into the soldiers, but shot them from behind the hills.

---

[21]The individual described was probably not Gen. Custer. Although the latter may have worn a buckskin outfit on June 25, it is a fact that both of his brothers were dressed similarly, while at least five other officers who fell with him may have worn a buckskin jacket. It is true that a melancholy reflection by Custer's long-time orderly, John Burkman, reveals an image of Custer wearing a white hat, fringed buckskin coat, and a red cravat while galloping away at noon, June 25. But sequential evidence about Custer's apparel seems to suggest a different picture. One source of evidence is provided by the Ree Indian scout, Soldier, who told Walter Camp that Custer took off his buckskin coat and tied it behind his saddle. There can be no doubt that this observation was made hours after Burkman's because it occurred near the lower forks of Reno Creek. The validity of Soldier's statement received a boost from Lt. Charles A. DeRudio, who attested to having seen both Gen. Custer and Lt. Cooke near Reno Hill, the identification made possible through their clothing—a blue shirt and buck-skin pants—the only officers to wear such a combination. Moreover, Peter Thompson, a survivor of Troop C, gained his last view of Custer north of Reno Hill, and he described Custer as an alert man, dressed in a shirt, buckskin pants tucked in his boots, and buckskin jacket fastened to the rear of his saddle. We may therefore conclude from these corroborating sources that the clothing pillaged from Custer's body consisted of a blue shirt and fringed buckskin pants, and that the man fully clad in buckskin was either Boston Custer or his brother, Captain Thomas W. Custer. See Graham, *The Custer Myth*, 345; Glendolin D. Wagner, *Old Neutriment* (New York, 1973), 151, 155; Hammer, *Custer in '76*, 188; Graham, *Abstract of the Official Record*, 115; and Magnussen, *Peter Thompson's Narrative*, 145-146.

[22]According to Gen. Edward S. Godfrey, George Custer carried two self-cocking, white-handled Bulldog pistols of English make. Godfrey added further that all sabres were left at the supply depot on the Yellowstone. See John S. du Mont, *Custer Battle Guns* (Ft. Collins, 1974), 96, 98; and also Hammer, *Custer in '76*, 87.

White Bull's son, Mad Wolf or Limber Bones, charged among the soldiers and was killed.[24]

[Editorial note: The following addendum is housed in the George B. Grinnell Collection, Item 463, Braun Research Library. It is included here because it shed additional light on the fate of Capt. Thomas W. Custer.]

Incident of [the] Custer Fight

For many years, I [George Grinnell] have been told with much mystery of the stripping of a white man on the Custer field, the man having been dressed in a buckskin coat, high boots, red handkerchief about the neck and tattoo marks on wrist. This man was probably Tom Custer. I never heard who it was that stripped him, until July 1914, when it came out that it was Little Horse. The party that was stripped was found southwest of where the monument [now] stands at the foot of a little hill. The man seemed to me an officer of the gray horse troops. Some of the Sioux said, "This is the man who brought the soldiers," and then the Sioux women smashed his head with mauls. The man had been scalped.[25]

---

[23]The mutilation of Tom Custer's remains was of such extent that identification would have been impossible if not for the letters "TWC" tattooed on a gunshot-shattered arm. See Hardorff, *Custer Battle Casualties*, 98-99. See also Marquis, *Wooden Leg*, 239, which describes another soldier, buckskin-clad, also with tattoos. This unfortunate victim was later decapitated, which might possibly explain the fate of Lt. Henry M. Harrington, declared MIA, who wore fringed canvas trousers. See du Mont, *Custer Battle Guns*, 97-98.

[24]White Shield was mistaken. Limber Bones, perhaps also known as Mad Wolf, was *not* White Bull's son, although an individual by this name was indeed slain at the Little Bighorn. The name of White Bull's son was Sounds the Ground as He Walks, or Noisy Walker, better known as Noisy Walking. The latter was mortally wounded in Deep Ravine. See Hardorff, *Hokahey! A Good Day to Die!*, 76-77.

[25]The remains of Tom Custer were found just below the top of Custer Hill, some twenty feet east of his brother, George Custer. Tom Custer was lying on his face and hands, his back riddled with arrows, several penetrating the head, the metal point of one bending on impact, making its extraction impossible. The cranium was broken by repeated blows from a blunt object to the back of the head, caving in the skull and decimating its facial features which were macerated further by decomposition. His throat was cut, and he was scalped,

the skin having been removed to his ears. One of his arms was broken by a gunshot, and all limbs bore slash marks, while his stomach was cut crosswise and lengthwise, causing the protrusion of the entrails. Identification of the remains was only possible through the letters "TWC" tattooed on one of his arms. See Hardorff, *Custer Battle Casualties*, 98-105.

Little Horse was a Northern Cheyenne who was born of a Crow woman. He was known as a very brave man who had been a Contrary and who had the honor to lead the assault in the Fetterman Fight of 1866. See Grinnell, *The Fighting Cheyennes*, 241.

The Little Hawk Interview

INTRODUCTION

Born in the 1840s, Little Hawk was the son of the renowned Cheyenne, Gentle Horse. Little Hawk participated in numerous skirmishes with the whites, among which the Beecher Island Fight and the Carpenter Fight, both in 1868, the Battle of Summit Springs in 1869, and the Battle of the Rosebud and Custer fight in 1876. He was known among the Cheyennes for his sense of humor, and had a reputation of being a practical joker.

This interview was conducted in 1908. I have extracted only that segment dealing with the Custer Fight, which is identified as Item 348, Field Notebook, 1908. The comments regarding the transcription of the previous interviews apply to this document as well.

THE LITTLE HAWK INTERVIEW
Northern Cheyenne Indian Reservation, 1908

The first charge was made by troops who went down Reno Creek and crossed the Little Horn. [They] went down the Little Horn about two miles and halted and went down into a low place where water used to stand and where there is timber among the lodges of one of the villages.[1] The Cheyennes charged him [Reno] and he did not stand but charged through them, going back the way he had come. He did not cross where he had come [from], but jumped over a bank. When he crossed, the Cheyennes did not follow him, for looking back they saw another lot of soldiers coming, and they went back to meet them. Little Hawk went back towards Custer. He does not know what became of Reno.

Little Hawk went back toward Custer and rode up the little ravine which the Indians went up in approaching Custer. The first thing he saw was Chief Comes in Sight[2] on a bobtail horse, riding up and down in front of the soldiers who were firing at him. Contrary Belly and Yellow Nose made the first charge. The two rode part way toward the soldiers and turned their horses and came back. The soldiers were all dismounted to fight on foot. As these two came back, an officer was killed and fell from his horse, and then all the soldiers mounted.

Yellow Nose and Contrary Belly now made a second

---

[1]Along with the Hunkpapas camped a small number of Blackfoot and Two Kettle Lakotas, and although it is generally assumed that Reno attacked the Hunkpapas, he actually hit the Blackfoot whose lodges were erected on the southern side of the circle. See the interview with Pretty White Buffalo Woman in Graham, *The Custer Myth*, 183; Flying By Interview, 1912, Walter Camp Manuscripts, Indiana University Library, 348; and White Bull Interview (1932), notebook 24.

[2]Born about 1849, Chief Comes in Sight was a revered Southern Cheyenne. However, although he may have possessed all the qualities of a chief, he did not hold such office, the word "chief" being part of his given name. Around 1870, Chief Comes in Sight eloped with Pemmican Woman, daughter of Chief Iron Shirt. Since she had married against her brother's wishes, it was rumored that this brother subsequently threw his life away out of shame, and that her father had disowned her. Although Grinnell states that Chief Comes in Sight was still alive in 1915, other sources report the year of his death as 1882. After her husband's death, Pemmican Woman travelled to Montana to ask her father to once again accept her as his daughter. However, the old man refused to see her, stating he never had a daughter. For biographical data on Chief Comes in Sight, see Grinnell, *The Cheyenne Indians*, I, 157, II, 44; Marquis, *Cheyennes and Sioux*, 16; Llewellyn and Hoebel, *The Cheyenne Way*, 174-75; Marquis, *Wooden Leg*, 211, 301, 329-30; and Grinnell, *The Fighting Cheyennes*, 336.

charge and were followed by the rest of the Indians. When they charged, the soldiers ran and went along the straight ridge[3] where they chased them like buffalo, and as long as they had their backs toward the Indians, the Indians rode right in among them. At the knoll where the monument [now] stands, the soldiers turned and that is the last place he saw them. White Bull's son and —[illegible] Black[4] fell right in among the soldiers as they were going along. White Bull's son lived till the next day. Twenty-three dead.[5]

Upon this round knoll the soldiers, having tied their horses in fours, let them go and they scattered, most of them running down toward the Little Horn. One company of soldiers went down toward the Little Horn and all but one man dismounted. The man who did not dismount rode away. He was riding a sorrel horse and Indians began to shoot at him, but could not hit him nor overtake him. At last, when he was almost out of shot, a ball hit him and knocked him off his horse. He is the only men who has not a stone [marker].

In the charge up the ridge where soldiers and Indians were together (where White Bull's son and —B[lack] were killed) not many soldiers were slain. Most of them got upon the knoll where the monument now stands. From there the most of them were killed by Indians hidden behind the little ridge, but there was some charging into these troops by Indians. Yellow Nose captured from a soldier a flag which had a gilt lance head on the staff, the only one of this kind taken. About fifteen flags were captured.[6]

---

[3]The "straight ridge" is probably Custer Ridge.

[4]The fading caused by the passing of time and Grinnell's peculiar longhand has rendered the transcription of the name partially illegible. The second Cheyenne casualty was Lame White Man who apparently was known also as Black Body.

[5]The actual body count was thirty-one males, of which seven were Cheyenne casualties. See Hardorff, *Hokahey! A Good Day to Die!*, 150-51.

[6]For an informative article on the Seventh's guidons, headquarters flag, and the regimental standard, see William A. Graham, "Custer's Battle Flags," *The* (Los Angeles) *Westerners Brand Book*, 1950 (Los Angeles, 1951):121-34.

The John Two Moons Interview

For biographical information on John Two Moons, see the Stanley Vestal interview with Young Two Moons in the section of miscellaneous interviews hereafter.

The Grinnell interview was conducted in 1908. I have extracted only that segment which deals with the Custer Fight and which is identified as Item 348, Field Notebook, 1908. The comments regarding the transcription of the previous interviews apply to this document as well.

THE JOHN TWO MOONS INTERVIEW
Northern Cheyenne Indian Reservation, 1908

John Two Moons was three miles from where the [Custer] fight took place and saw it all, but did not take part in it. His account should therefore give a good general idea of what took place. When he first saw the soldiers they were just coming down the steep hill east of the battlefield. They were on a lope and Indians were behind them, but they paid no attention to them. This was Custer's command. He saw nothing of Reno's battle. It was out of his sight.

After the soldiers turned upon the little ridge, the Gray Horse Company stopped where [the present] monument is. The others went on, stopping at intervals until there were four lines, the last opposite to the camp. After they saw soldiers there, [John] Two Moons, who was nearer to the river on a hillside, ran with others and caught their horses and rushed toward the fight. Several charges had been made but no fighting had been done. Indians were struggling up the gulch northeast of the soldiers like ants rushing out of a hill.[1]

Yellow Nose made two dashes toward the soldiers and returned, and said to his people, "Let us charge." The third company — the one toward the river — had moved back a little toward the second. The Indians were trying to drive the three companies on this ridge, running about north and south,[2] over to the Gray Horse Company. Yellow Nose made a third charge, but the other Indians did not follow him.

Meantime, the Indians were getting further to the north, trying to surround the soldiers. At the fourth charge, on Yellow Nose's orders, all Indians mounted and Yellow Nose made a charge, and all Indians followed. They crowded the company furthest north [south?] and they started to run down the ridge. As they got down part way toward the Gray Horse Company, the latter began to fire and drove the Indians off, and the soldiers reached the Gray Horse Company.

Some [soldiers] were killed, however, when they reached the Gray Horse [Company]. The latter shot at the Indians so fast that they drove the Indians back out of sight over the hill

---

[1] This statement apparently has reference to Deep Coulee. For a possible explanation of the confusion surrounding compass locations, see Fox, *Archaeology, History, and Custer's Last Battle*, 150.

[2] The "north and south" ridge is probably the present Custer Ridge. For further clarification, the reader is referred to the map reproduced in the Young Two Moons interview with Stanley Vestal.

toward the [location of the present Crow] agency. The same Indians called out very loud, "All dismount," and they did so. It was done quickly. When the Indians dismounted, they shot at soldiers who retreated for the top of the hill. Then the Indians mounted and charged. Then the Gray Horse Company turned their horses loose, and some of the horses rushed through the Indians and toward the river.

When the Indians charged to the top of the hill, they saw the other two companies way down near to the river. Then all the soldiers turned their horses loose. The Gray Horse Company was destroyed on the hill near where they went out of sight. The Indians charged in among them. One of the companies retreated down toward a little gulch where they tried to fight under cover. Here the last of the soldiers were killed.[3] He saw and heard what the Gray Horse Company did, and [what] those [did] who took refuge in the little creek. Those in the creek were all killed before he got there.

If these soldiers had all stood together, the Indians could have done nothing with them. The yelling of the Indians seemed to frighten the cavalry horses and they were naying and — [plunging?] so that the men could not handle their guns. If the horses, after they had been turned loose, had come to a shallow place in the Little Horn River, they would have crossed it and no one knows when they would have stopped. [However,] they struck a deep hole in the river and could not get out on the other side, and stayed there swimming around.

---

[3] The "little gulch" or "creek" is present Deep Ravine where twenty-eight soldiers were slain.

The Camp Interviews

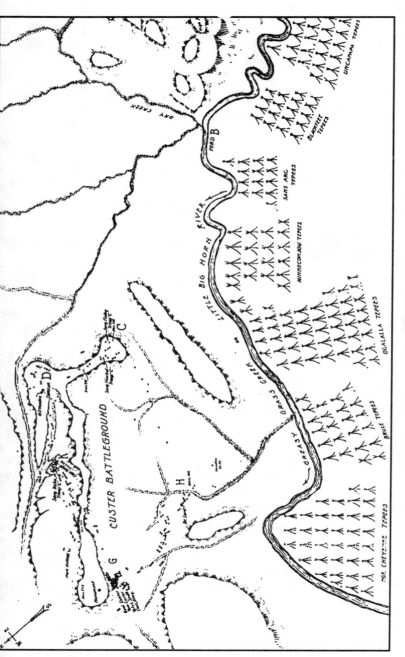

DRAWN BY WALTER M. CAMP IN 1908 AND UPDATED IN LATER YEARS

This survey map of the battlefield was based on information provided by Maj. McDougall, Sgt. Kanipe and other survivors of the fight. The dots represent markers erected at the kill sites of the slain.

Courtesy of Custer Battlefield National Monument, National Park Service.

Walter Mason Camp

Like George B. Grinnell, Walter Mason Camp had an enduring interest in the Plains Indians and their wars. Born in Campstown, Pennsylvania, in 1867, Walter Camp entered a career in railway service in 1883, which would span a period of some forty years. Graduating from Pennsylvania State College in 1891, he became an engineer to the Rainier Avenue Electric Railway in Seattle, Washington, and was promoted to superintendent a few years later. In 1897, he became the editor of the *Railway and Engineering Review,* which position he served until his sudden death in 1925.

Camp devoted the last twenty years of his life to avocational research on the American Indian wars. Known to his Lakota friends by the name of *Wicati* (Camp), he was described as a quiet, unassuming man who was highly respected for his talents and knowledge. Camp seemed to have had a tireless pen, an intense interest in the Western Indians, and an indefatigable will to pursue the historical truth. During the course of his research, he established a legacy for himself and those he interviewed, which will forever live in the annals of the American Indian history.

By 1925, Camp had completed a chapter outline of his manuscript for his publisher. However, his untimely death the same year delayed publication half a century, until 1976, when only a small part of it was made available through the Brigham Young University Press. Of the four Camp interviews which follow, the interviews with Tall Bull and White Bull are reproduced by permission from the Brigham Young University Library, while the interviews with Bull Hump and Little Wolf are published by permission from the Indiana University Library.

The Tall Bull Interview

INTRODUCTION

For biographical information on Tall Bull, see the introduction to his interview with Grinnell. Camp's interview with Tall Bull is found in the Walter Mason Camp Collection, Interviews, Box 4, Brigham Young University Library. However, due to Camp's handwriting style, in addition to the fading caused by the passing of time, and the fragility of the original documents, I have used the transcript prepared by Dr. Kenneth Hammer who included it in *Custer in '76*, pages 212-213.

THE TALL BULL INTERVIEW
Lamedeer, Montana, July 22, 1910
Thaddeus Red Water, Interpreter

Tall Bull (Hotuga Kastatche), 57 years old. Crook's fight [on] 3/17/76 was with Cheyenne camp [which contained] only few Sioux lodges.[1] Most of Cheyennes wintered 75/76 [on] lower Powder—down near Yellowstone. When [we] fought Crook [on] 6/17/76, our camp was at lone tepee.[2]

---

[1] The Cheyenne camp contained ten Oglala lodges, of which eight belonged to He Dog's Northern Oglala band. See Marshall, "How Many Indians Were There?," 210, 211.

[2] The term "lone tepee" has reference to a Lakota funeral lodge which stood on the north side of Reno Creek, about four miles from the Little Bighorn, on a wide and smooth section of ground which gently sloped toward the creek. See Hammer, *Custer in '76*, 155-156.

THIS PHOTOGRAPH OF TALL BULL AT AGE 61, WAS TAKEN BY D.L. GILL
in 1914 during a Cheyenne delegation visit to Washington, D.C.
Photo courtesy of Smithsonian Institution, National Anthropological Archives.

When heard [of] soldiers to south [of us], we left the
women and children in camp and traveled all night and
reached headwaters of Rosebud about daylight next morning. Did not follow up Crook because thought [we] had done
enough for one day and did not know Crook [was] in such a
bad fix. Did not expect soldiers would follow us as far as Little Bighorn.

Cheyennes call Little Bighorn [the] Goat River.
Cheyenne village at north end of camp just as I [Walter
Camp] have it. Tall Bull says there were 3,000 population in
Cheyenne village. Head chiefs Little Bighorn: Two Moons,
White Bull, and Lame White Man, who was killed. Only
part of Cheyennes and Sioux got into Reno fight in bottoms.
Cheyennes did not learn [that] soldiers [were] coming until
Reno attacked. The Sioux must have known of approach of
soldiers, but Cheyennes did not.[3]

After returning from Reno, women going over east to get
on high ground to overlook Reno fight discovered Custer
coming. Custer got onto flat near Ford B [see map on page
70] within easy gunshot of village, and Indians drove him
back.[4] By [the] time I got there, [Indians] had driven soldiers
to first rise (where [Corp. John] Foley lay), and they were
going up the ridge to right of Custer Coulee and Indians driving them.[5]

---

[3]Moments before Reno's attack, the southern camps were alerted of the danger by blanket signals from the bluffs across the river. At the same time, it was learned that a young
Lakota had been killed by troops descending Reno Creek. See Graham, *The Custer Myth*,
84; and also Stanley Vestal, *Sitting Bull, Champion of the Sioux* (Norman, 1957), 160.

[4]The term "Ford B" first appeared on Custer Battlefield maps drawn in 1876 under the
supervision of Lt. Edward Maguire, Corps of Engineers. This military term identified present Medicine Tail Ford, which was known in the early days as Minneconjou Ford for the
Lakota band whose lodges stood here on June 25.

[5]The body of Corp. John Foley of C Troop was found on June 28, on a little rise near the
mouth of Medicine Tail Coulee, some 1,100 feet from the crossing. See Hardorff, *Custer
Battle Casualties*, 113-114. The present name for Custer Coulee is Deep Coulee, which is
not to be confused with Deep *Ravine* which runs on the north side of Calhoun Ridge.

The men who had no horses to go to Reno, first began the attack on Custer, and I did not see the first of it. Soldiers did not make any charge on Indians during the Custer fight. He [Tall Bull] is very clear that Custer was driven farther and farther back from river. Soldiers fell back from river, some mounted and some on foot and not in very good order. Heard the volleys. The first was at the beginning of fight at "C" ([Sgt. Jeremiah] Finley marker). The last was at "G".[6] Gray horses all mixed up with bays.

I was near "H" and heard a big war whoop that soldiers were coming. Soldiers came on foot and ran right through us into deep gully, and this was the last of the fight, and the men were killed in this gully.[7] Tall Bull says that some of the men who ran from the edge of the ridge to the gully were firing their guns at random.[8] Tall Bull has been several times on the battlefield in recent years and knows ground well and is apparently honest in his statements.

After Little Bighorn [fight, we] went up Little Bighorn to near Sheridan and across to Rosebud and down Rosebud and across to point about 18 miles below Lamedeer, and across to Tongue and down Powder to near mouth, and then to north side of Black Hills, and then crossed Little Missouri and

---

[6]The body of Sgt. Jeremiah Finley, also of C Troop, was found on the west end of Calhoun Ridge, on June 27. See Hardorff, *Custer Battle Casualties*, 112-113. The initial volley firing took place on a high ridge one mile east of the ford. Known as Nye-Cartwright Ridge, this location yielded more than two hundred casings near its crest, many lying in groups of threes. These groupings, and the spacing between them, revealed that three volleys had been fired in mounted line formation. See Greene, "Evidence and the Custer Enigma," 20-22; and also Hardorff, *Markers*, 37.

[7]Reference is made to the slayings in Deep Ravine. For additional evidence that these slayings occurred at the end of the fight, see, for example, the Camp interviews in Hardorff, *Lakota Recollections*.

[8]The same sentiment was expressed by the Oglala, Bear Lying Down, who told Walter Camp that these soldiers had discarded their carbines and used revolvers which they fired into the air, without taking aim. See Hardorff, *Markers*, 60.

went back to Powder and up Crazy Woman's Fork and then broke up, some of [the] Indians going north...[9]

---

[9]For a reconstruction of these movements by the allied Indian force, see Gray, *Centennial Campaign*, 338-344.

The White Bull Interview

INTRODUCTION

For biographical information on White Bull, see the introduction to his interview with Grinnell (pages 37-39). Camp's interview with White Bull in 1910 was probably the last interview given by this renowned Cheyenne, who passed away the same year. The interview is found in the Walter Mason Camp Collection, Interviews, Box 2, Brigham Young University Library. Due to Camp's handwriting style, in addition to the fading caused by the passing of time, and the fragility of the original documents, I have used the transcript prepared by Dr. Kenneth Hammer who included it in *Custer in '76*, page 211.

THE WHITE BULL INTERVIEW

Northern Cheyenne Indian Reservation, Montana,
 July 23, 1910
Thaddeus Red Water, Interpreter

White Bull (75 years old)...was in fight of 3/17/76. [This was] a Cheyenne camp under Willow Brushes [and contained] only a few Sioux.[1] Wintered on Tongue towards

---

[1]Willow Bushes was the leader of a small band of Cheyennes. After the surrender in 1877, he went south with Little Chief in 1878, and resettled in Oklahoma Territory.

spring when [they] moved to Powder. Camp at time of Crook's fight was near second fork of Reno Creek. There were some white rocky bluffs there.² His horse gave out, and he did not get to Crook fight, but saw it at a distance. Did not pursue Crook because ponies [were] worn out. One Cheyenne was killed and another wounded in this fight.³

Did not learn of approach of soldiers until Reno attacked. Did not get into Custer fight until it was nearly over. Says (and so does Tall Bull) that many of Custer's soldiers acted like men intoxicated or beside themselves, as they fired into the air without taking aim.⁴ Did not try to crush Reno [on

---

²The White Buttes are located on the north side of Reno Creek, just below the point where the South Fork meets the Middle Fork, some four miles east of the Little Bighorn. The Indian camp stood on the north side of the creek and just below the White Buttes, and it extended for about a half mile downstream. See Hammer, *Custer in '76*, 155-156.

³According to Wooden Leg, the name of this slain Cheyenne was Black Sun. This man had painted his body yellow and wore a stuffed weasel on top of his head for protective power. Apparently, Black Sun was shot through the body from behind and died that same night. This is probably the same man spoken of by the Minneconjou, White Bull, who dragged this man back to safety, for which act he was later honored by the Cheyennes. Because of the yellow paint, White Bull may have thought that the Cheyenne's name was Sunrise, but he recalled that some Lakotas remembered this victim's name as Water Dog, probably mistaking the stuffed weasel for an otter. However, Walter Campbell's field notes of the White Bull interview indicate that the Cheyenne's name was Alligator. Yet another name for this slain Cheyenne was given by John Stands in Timber who identified him as Scabby. According to Stands in Timber, this man died three days after the battle from the effects of a gunshot to the abdomen and was buried at the mouth of Prairie Dog Creek. See Marquis, *Wooden Leg*, 202; Stanley Vestal, *Warpath, the True Story of the Fighting Sioux, Told in a Biography of Chief White Bull* (Lincoln, 1984), 189; the White Bull Interview, Walter Campbell Collection, Box 105, Notebook 24, University of Oklahoma Library; John Stands in Timber and Margot Liberty, *Cheyenne Memories* (Lincoln, 1972), 187.

⁴Perhaps the Lakotas later provided the best explanation of the strange behavior of the Custer soldiers. The Hunkpapa, Shoots Walking, recalled that the soldiers acted as though they were drunk; that they did not seem to know how to shoot; that many of them threw their guns down; and that they fought without any system whatsoever. This opinion was shared by Red Horse, a Minneconjou, who stated that Custer's soldiers became foolish, and that many threw away their guns and raised their hands in a sign of surrender. Bear Lying down, an Oglala, remembered that Custer's troopers fired wildly into the air and acted as if intoxicated, which agrees with the statement of his tribesman, He Dog, who distinctly

Reno Hill] because thought could starve him out and in this way [would] not lose men recklessly charging the fortifications which protected the soldiers, and [they] did not know how many soldiers were there. When Terry approached [they] thought had better retire. Says the Cheyennes had about 200 tepees and about 3,000 people.

---

recalled that some of the soldiers feigned death by playing possum, but that none were drunk. Two Bulls, a Yanktonais Nakota, compared the behavior of Custer's troopers with that of boys, while Standing Bear, the father of Luther, found very little honor in fighting such frightened adversaries. See Walter Campbell Collection, Box 111; Graham, *The Custer Myth*, 62; Walter Camp Manuscripts, Transcripts, 269; Edward A. Milligan, *High Noon on the Greasy Grass* (Bottineau, 1972), no pagination; Luther Standing Bear, *My People the Sioux* (Lincoln, 1975), 83. Reviewing this evidence, there exists little doubt that the strange behavior displayed by Custer's troopers was caused by fear. This erratic behavior resulted in a breakdown of military discipline which was duly noted by the Indians.

The Bull Hump and White Bird Interview

INTRODUCTION

Born about 1848, Bull Hump was the son of Chief Dull Knife and Pawnee Woman. Bull Hump was prominently mentioned in the defense of his father's village during Col. MacKenzie's attack in 1876. During this battle, a wounded but defiant Bull Hump helped the women and little children flee to safety. However, his brother, Little Hump, was instantly killed by a gunshot fired by Frank North. His brother's death was avenged by the slaying of Lt. John A. McKinney, on whose body Bull Hump counted coup.

During the outbreak of Dull Knife's imprisoned band at Fort Robinson in 1879, tragedy struck his family again. During the escape, Bull Hump's younger sister, Princess, was shot to death while shielding several young children with her own body against the soldiers' bullets.

Prior to his father's death in 1883, Bull Hump was chosen by him and the whole tribe to be the principal chief. However, Bull Hump refused to accept the hereditary position of his father on the grounds that by 1883, tribal chiefs were no longer an absolute necessity for the survival of the tribe. Later, however, Bull Hump did become a chief, but not as his father's successor. Bull Hump was still alive as late as 1928.

Biographical information on White Bird is scarce. He fought in both the Rosebud Fight and the Custer Battle. In the latter fight, he received a gunshot in the leg which caused him to limp the remainder of his life. White Bird lived between Lame Deer and Busby and died a very respected man.

The original text of this interview is contained in the Walter Mason Camp Manuscripts, Indiana University Library. Due to Camp's handwriting style, in addition to the fading caused by the passing of time, and the fragility of the original documents, I have used the transcript prepared by Dr. Kenneth Hammer. This consists of pages 366-368, to which I have added paragraphing and punctuation.

THE BULL HUMP AND WHITE BIRD INTERVIEW
Northern Cheyenne Indian Reservation, Montana, 1912
Willis Rowland [Interpreter]

Hump [is] sixty-four years old.... Hump's name is Bull Hump. Yes, Hump was at Little Bighorn. Two Moons was chief warrior because of the absence of other chiefs. Wild Hog was there, but Dull Knife was at Red Cloud Agency, as well as Little Chief.[1]

The chiefs in villages that Crook attacked March 17, 1876, were Willow Bushes and Two Moons. [They] got some of the horses back from Reynolds [on the] first night. Started out to recover more on the second night and found where soldiers had killed them.[2]

[On the day of the Sibley skirmish] the Indians were running buffalo all over the country, and while doing this, a small party of Cheyennes ran upon the trail of the scouts and followed it to the timber. They fired into the timber a little

---

[1] For information on Two Moons, see the Two Moons interviews hereafter. Wild Hog was a war chief of the Northern Cheyenne Elk Society. He participated in all the northern engagements with the U.S. Military, including the Battle of the Little Bighorn. Although relocated in Indian Territory, he came north with Dull Knife's band in 1878, and surren-

while and High Bear, a cousin of Hump, was killed.[3] Toward night they left the place after recovering High Bear's body, and some Sioux came upon the place the next day and got the [abandoned] horses tied to the trees. Hump never heard that any of these horses had been killed.[4]

Custer's camp on night of June 24 was on the flat at Busby

dered at Fort Robinson. Wild Hog was a defiant man who, when taken to the guardhouse at Fort Robinson in 1879, attempted suicide with a butcher knife rather than be imprisoned. Wild Hog died among the Lakotas on Pine Ridge where he lies buried. See Grinnell, *The Fighting Cheyennes*, 234, 404, 417; and also Marquis, *Wooden Leg*, 211, 218.

Dull Knife was one of four principle civil leaders of the Northern Cheyennes. He had been a war chief, and although known as a brave and skilled fighter, it was said that he was neither an organizer nor a planner of his battles. In 1876, Dull Knife's village was destroyed by Col. Ranald S. MacKenzie, which led to the surrender and subsequent removal of his band to Indian Territory in 1877. However, due to deplorable health conditions in the south, he led his band on an epic trek to their northern homeland the following year and surrendered at Fort Robinson. Being imprisoned and subjected to starvation, Dull Knife's people attempted to make their escape, with disastrous results. Of the 150 people of his band, some seventy men, women, and children were indiscriminately killed as the immediate result of an incompetent post commander and the inhumanity of the War Department. Dull Knife died in 1883, a broken-hearted old man who was haunted by the memories of the slaughter of his people, among whom were a son and a daughter. See Grinnell, *The Cheyenne Indians*, II, 51, 421; Grinnell, *The Fighting Cheyennes*, 364, 422. For a stirring account of the Cheyenne exodus from Oklahoma, see Mari Sandoz, *Cheyenne Autumn* (New York, 1953).

Established along the White River in northwestern Nebraska in 1873, Red Cloud Agency was a distribution center for annuity goods granted to the Oglalas. It was operative until 1877, when it was relocated along the Missouri River.

Little Chief was a Southern Cheyenne leader of a Dog Soldier band. Gifted with the persuasive power of oration, he negotiated the surrender of his band and several others to General Miles in 1877. The same year his people were moved to Indian Territory, but in 1881, his band was allowed to resettle among the Oglalas on Pine Ridge with whom many of the Dog Soldiers had marital ties. However, due to the Cheyennes' army service during the Sioux War and the Ghost Dance troubles, Lakota resentment against their presence grew, and in 1891, Little Chief's band was finally allowed to rejoin their kinsmen on the Tongue River Reservation in Montana. Little Chief died near Birney in 1906. See Hyde, *Life of George Bent*, 122; Grinnell, *The Fighting Cheyennes*, 401; Mark H. Brown and W.R. Felton, *The Frontier Years: L.A. Huffman, Photographer of the Plains* (new York, 1955), 99, 101.

[2]Of the herd of seven hundred ponies, the Indians recaptured some five hundred. The balance was further reduced by the intentional slaughter of some one hundred by the military, the remainder being taken to Fort Laramie. See J.W. Vaughn, *The Reynolds Campaign on Powder River* (Norman, 1961), 112, 153.

schoolhouse, perhaps near the preacher's house ([Rev. G.A.] Linscheid).[5] Little Wolf and a small band of Cheyennes (thirty or forty) had left Red Cloud Agency and were hunting for the hostile camp. They supposed they would find it on the Rosebud and [they] went through the mountains to Muddy Creek and down it. When one of their scouts got down near the mouth of it, he saw soldiers passing up the Rosebud and rode back and so informed Little Wolf.[6] The Cheyenne then struck westward through the hills and came out into the valley of the Rosebud about where Ridge Walker now lives.[7] They put scouts out to watch Custer and went back and camped at mouth of Muddy. The Cheyenne scouts watched Custer's movements all night and followed him when the command moved on. Little Wolf's camp followed in the morning up in the hills and kept watch of the soldiers, with a view to capture the pack animals. They did not get up in time to take part in the fighting of the first day....[8]

---

[3]On July 7, 1876, Lt. Frederick W. Sibley, Second Cavalry, and a detachment of twenty-five troopers and four civilians encountered a Cheyenne force near the headwaters of the Little Bighorn which nearly succeeded in capturing the entire command. After a short fight, Sibley abandoned his horses and escaped on foot. The only casualty was High Bear, or Tall Bear, who was better known to the whites by his Lakota name White Antelope. For an eyewitness account, see John F. Finerty, *War-path and Bivouac* (Norman, 1961), 113-128.

[4]The horses were accidentally discovered by a hunting party of Hunkpapas. According to Has Horns, these were exceptionally fine horses which were used to run races against those captured in the Custer fight. Round Clown and Shoots the Enemy, both Hunkpapas, each obtained two of the Sibley horses. It was said that the latter thus acquired one of the best race horses the Hunkpapas ever had. Camp Manuscripts, 355-356.

[5]The Linscheid residence stood on the NE40, Section 31, Township 3 South, Range 39, East Montana Meridian, about 200 yards south of the Rosebud Creek. According to Cheyenne informants, Custer's camp on June 24 was located on the riverbank, a little northeast of the Linscheid residence. H.E. Morrow to Walter Camp, 4/12 and 4/28/1912, Walter Mason Camp Papers, Denver Public Library.

[6]For data on Little Wolf, see the Little Wolf interview hereafter.

[7]Ridge Walker was a prominent Cheyenne shaman. It was said that he could paralyze and kill animals and human beings at a great distance, and that he could even make himself disappear while seated under a buffalo robe. See Thomas B. Marquis, *Cheyennes and Sioux*, 34.

At the Little Bighorn Two Moons and Walking White Man were the chiefs, and Walking White Man was killed.[9] Two Moons and Willow Bushes were the chiefs in the village that Crook broke up on March 17, 1876. Bull Hump says they recaptured part of their ponies the first night (March 17), and on second night they repeated the trick and got back more of them. They kept hanging around after Crook and finally found where Crook had killed the uncaptured balance of the herd.

---

[8]While following Custer's trail up the Rosebud, three Cheyenne scouts—Big Crow Black Horse and Medicine Bull—were fired upon by a detail of four troopers led by Sgt. William A. Curtiss, who had returned on the trail to recover a "personals" bag. See Hardorff, *Hokahey! A Good Day to Die!*, 27-28.

[9]Better known as Lame White Man, this individual was the head soldier of the Elk Society and a man of much influence among the Northern Cheyennes. Some distances south of the present monument, he charged furiously among the troopers and was killed by a gunshot wound to the chest. See Hardorff, *Hokahey! A Good Day to Die!*, 65-69.

THIS PHOTOGRAPH OF YOUNG LITTLE WOLF AT ABOUT 78 YEARS OF AGE
was taken by G.J. McMurry during the 50th anniversary of the Custer Battle in
1926. Known in his younger years as Red Bird, he later took the name of his
famous uncle and was listed on the agency rolls as Laban Little Wolf.
Photo courtesy of Custer Battlefield National Monument, National Park Service.

The Little Wolf Interview

INTRODUCTION

Born about 1848, Young Little Wolf was the son of Big Left Hand, and was a maternal nephew of the renowned Chief Little Wolf who had married his mother's sister. Known during his youth as Thorny Tree, he was given the name Red Bird upon reaching adolescence. However, during a battle with Shoshones in the late 1870s he was heralded for his valorous conduct, and in recognition of his nephew's bravery, Chief Little Wolf later bestowed his own name on him. After the surrender of the Cheyennes, Young Little Wolf was sent to Indian Territory, but in 1878, he came north with Little Wolf's band. Instead of going to Fort Keogh with his uncle, Young Little Wolf and a small following surrendered at Pine Ridge and he eventually became a tribal chief.

In 1886, Young Little Wolf was involved in one of the last intertribal skirmishes when he killed several men of a Crow horse-stealing party who were trapped near the confluence of Hay Creek and Tongue River. In 1906, he was interviewed by Dr. Joseph K. Dixon on the grounds of historic Fort Custer, but, unfortunately, this interview was not included in Dixon's publication. Although Young Little Wolf eventually was elected as tribal leader of all the Northern Cheyennes, throughout his later life the whites mistook him for his famous uncle. Listed on the agency rolls as Laban Little Wolf, he passed away in 1927.

The original text of this interview is contained in the Walter Mason Camp Manuscripts, Indiana University. Due to Camp's handwriting style, in addition to the fading caused by the passing of time, and the fragility of the original documents, I have used the transcript prepared by Dr. Kenneth Hammer, pages 632-633. For further clarification of Camp's text, the reader is referred to Camp's battlefield map on page 70.

THE LITTLE WOLF INTERVIEW
Northern Cheyenne Indian Reservation, Montana, 1918

When Custer was first seen he was opposite Ford "B" in Medicine Tail Coulee, travelling parallel with river, soldiers deployed and seemingly trying to circle the camp. After he passed Medicine Tail Coulee, Indians followed him. Only one [skirmish] line on Custer Ridge, [which] was from "C" to "D" [see map on page 70]. I was there. Lame White Man charged them here and chased them to Keogh where he (Lame White Man) was killed. From "D" and "G" no line, soldiers moving right along. We did not know it was Custer. After the fight we discussed the identity of the soldiers and all thought [it was] Crook.[1]

Little Wolf says day before the Sibley Scout many Cheyennes went into mountains to hunt. Bad Hand alias

---

[1] It is not certain whether Little Wolf viewed this scene from the south slope or the north slope of Calhoun Ridge. However, most of the Cheyennes concentrated on the north slope, and it was here—on the river side of the hogback now known as Custer Ridge—where Lame White Man eventually pressed the troops and where he was slain.

For evidence that Custer was identified, see the statement by the Cheyenne, Kate Big Head, in Marquis, *Custer on the Little Bighorn* (Lodi, 1967), 43. However, I attach very little credence to this statement because such information would have been common knowledge in the small Cheyenne community. However, no Cheyenne informant ever provided any such corroborating evidence. Indeed, the Cheyenne, Wooden Leg, another informant to Marquis, learned later from the Lakotas that they had fought Long Hair at the Little Bighorn. This Lakota informant, a Hunkpapa chief, said he was absolutely sure because he had killed Long Hair himself, recognizing him as Custer from his *long and wavy yellow hair!*

High Bear was killed. We left them and got horses next day....[2]

Little Wolf says High Back Wolf was the first Northern Cheyenne who ever went to Washington. He went with an ox train and was gone about a year. While he was gone so long, his people thought he must have died.[3] My name before I took my uncle's name was Red Bird. Little Wolf was about eighty years old when he died.[4] Dull Knife was older when he died, and he died first. Little Wolf past seventy [on] August 16, 1918....

Turkey Legs (Mahsinuwita) had about twenty lodges at Red Cloud [Agency] on June 25, 1876.[5] Little Wolf at Little Bighorn. Little Wolf says his people sent for Little Wolf to come and fight, and he came and was intending to talk to them against fighting, but Custer beat him there. When Sioux heard this they were all very angry and threatened to kill him.[6] Lame White Man was head chief at Little Bighorn

---

Of course, this Hunkpapa and others did not know that Custer had cropped his hair very short just before leaving on the expedition. See Marquis, *Wooden Leg*, 273.

[2]Bad Hand, or Crippled Hand, was the nickname for the Cheyenne better known to the whites by his Lakota name, White Antelope. This man was described as wearing a white buckskin outfit and a magnificent war bonnet and was considered to be an enterprising leader with many skills. He was killed by a gunshot while leading a charge against Sibley's force, the slaying being claimed by both Frank Grouard and Baptiste Pourier. See Joe DeBarthe, *Life of Frank Grouard* (Norman, 1958), 141; Finerty, *War-path and Bivouac*, 119; and also Donald F. Danker, "Big Bat Pourier's Version of the Sibley Scout," *Nebraska History* (Summer 1985): 129-143.

[3]High Back Wolf was a respected Cheyenne leader who went to Washington in 1831 as a member of the first Cheyenne delegation to ever visit the seat of American government. He and two other delegates, Limber Lance and Bull Head, returned in 1832. Later that same year, George Catlin painted High Back Wolf's portrait, but he identified his subject as Wolf on the Hill as a result of deficient translation. In 1833, High Back Wolf was mortally wounded while trying to intervene on behalf of some relatives in a dispute over a stolen wife. In the same year a meteor shower occurred, and it was said among the Cheyennes that surely the stars fell from the sky because of the death of such an important man. See Grinnell, *The Cheyenne Indians*, Vol.. I, 30; George Catlin, *Letters and Notes on the Manners, Customs, and Conditions of North American Indians* (New York, 1973), Vol.. II, 2; Donald J. Berthrong, *The Southern Cheyennes* (Norman, 1963), 78.

and not Two Moons. Lame White Man was killed there, says Little Wolf.

---

⁴Born in 1821, Little Wolf was a respected tribal chief, and a man of much influence since his early age when he was known as Two Tails. He had once been the head soldier of the Elk Society and as such had gained a reputation as a dominant leader who enjoyed the act of killing. He was a member of the Cheyenne delegation which visited Washington, D.C., in 1873. He did not partake in the Custer Battle and survived the disaster which befell Dull Knife's village, although wounded six times. After the relocation in Indian Territory in 1877, he led his band on an epic journey to their northern homeland in Montana and surrendered at Ft. Keogh in 1879, where he and members of his band enlisted as U.S. Indian Scouts. In 1883, Little Wolf went into voluntary exile after killing a tribesman in a dispute over his daughter, Pretty Walker. He passed away in 1904, and was buried on the north side of Muddy Creek, just above the residence of Bill Rowland. Through the thoughtful interference of his friend, George Grinnell, Little Wolf's remains were exhumed from their unmarked grave in 1928, and reinterred at the agency's cemetery, the new site marked by a headstone set by Grinnell to identify the final resting place of a great Cheyenne. See Grinnell, *The Cheyenne Indians*, 221; Hyde, *Life of George Bent*, 294, 349; and Marquis, *Wooden Leg*, 16, 17, 373. For a comprehensive account of Little Wolf, see Gary L. Roberts, "The Shame of Little Wolf," *Montana, The Magazine of Western History* (Summer 1978): 36-47.

⁵Turkey Leg was a Northern Cheyenne and a man who was considered to be of friendly disposition to the whites, with whom he preferred to be at peace. However, he and his band are chiefly remembered for their involvement in the derailment of a Union Pacific freight train in 1867, near Plum Creek Station, Nebraska, some sixty miles southeast of present North Platte. See Hyde, *Life of George Bent*, 273, 276; and also Grinnell, *The Fighting Cheyennes*, 263.

⁶See also Marquis, *Wooden Leg*, 248-252. Wooden Leg was Little Wolf's nephew and witnessed these events.

Interviews with Two Moons

TWO MOONS, DRESSED IN A MAGNIFICENT WARBONNET
This youthful photograph was taken by Laton A. Huffman
at Fort Keogh, Montana, in 1878.
Photo courtesy of Custer Battlefield National Monument, National Park Service.

Hamlin Garland's Interview with Two Moons

INTRODUCTION

Born in western Wyoming in 1842, Two Moons was the son of
Carries the Otter, an Arikara captive who married into the Northern Cheyenne tribe. Although often mistaken to mean the moon
itself, the name Two Moons merely denoted the Cheyenne way of
counting time, namely, two lunar months. At age fifteen, he witnessed the death of his father during a skirmish between
Cheyennes and Col. Edwin V. Sumner's force on the Solomon
Fork in Kansas.

Two Moons was a minor chief of the Fox Society, and although
he was absent in the Fetterman Fight of 1866, he participated in
nearly every other skirmish with the encroaching whites, including the Rosebud Battle and the Custer Fight of 1876. After the
surrender of the Cheyennes to Col. Nelson A. Miles in 1877, Two
Moons enlisted as a U.S. Indian Scout, and as a result of his pleas-
ant personality, his friendliness towards the whites, and his ability
to get along with the military, he was selected head chief by Miles,
which was later ratified by the Cheyennes.

Two Moons passed away in 1917. It was said that he had been
blind since the early 1900s, but that he miraculously had regained
his eyesight during the last few years of his life. Although his mili-

tary and political status has been the subject of some controversy, the fact remains that Two Moons was able to give some measure of direction and stability to his people during extremely difficult times. His sense of humor, displayed at the expense of the white man's gullibility, seems to suggest that he may have understood them far better than they had understood him.

Hamlin Garland's interview with Two Moons was originally published in *McClure's Magazine*, September 1898. The following is a verbatim transcript of the original, except that I have corrected some errors in grammar and spelling. The original publication also included a painted portrait of Two Moons, which is reproduced herein in black and white.

HAMLIN GARLAND'S INTERVIEW WITH TWO MOONS
Northern Cheyenne Indian Reservation, Montana, 1898

As we topped the low, pine-clad ridge and looked into the hot, dry valley, Wolf Voice, my Cheyenne interpreter, pointed at a little log cabin, toward the green line of alders wherein the Rosebud ran, and said: "His house—Two Moons."[1]

As we drew near we came to a puzzling fork in the road. The left branch skirted a corner of a wire fence, the right turned into a field. We started to the left, but the waving of a blanket in the hands of a man at the cabin door directed us to the right. As we drew nearer we perceived Two Moons spreading blankets in the scant shade of his low cabin. Some young Cheyennes were grinding a sickle. A couple of children were playing about the little log stables. The barnyard and buildings were like those of a white settler on the new

---

[1] Also known as Old Wolf Voice, this Cheyenne served as an interpreter to Lt. William P. Clark who negotiated the surrender of Little Wolf's band to Gen. Miles in 1878. In 1889, Wolf Voice enlisted in Lt. Edward Casey's troop of Cheyenne Indian Scouts and saw limited action during the Ghost Dance troubles at Pine Ridge in 1890. See Grinnell, *The Fighting Cheyennes*, 411; and also Harold McCracken, *Frederic Remington's Own West* (New York, 1960), 237.

CHIEF TWO MOON.
NORTHERN CHEYENNE.

TWO MOONS AS PAINTED BY E. A. BURBANK
This portrait illustrated Hamlin Garland's interview
and was published in *McClure's* magazine, September 1898.

and arid sod. It was all barren and unlovely—the home of poverty.

As we dismounted at the door, Two Moons came out to meet us with hand outstretched. "How," he said, with the heartiest, long-drawn note of welcome. He motioned us to be seated on the blankets which he had spread for us upon seeing our approach. Nothing could exceed the dignity and sincerity of his greeting.

As we took seats he brought out tobacco and a pipe. He was a tall old man, of a fine, clear brown complexion, big-chested, erect, and martial of bearing. His smiling face was broadly benignant, and his manners were courteous and manly.

While he cut his tobacco, Wolf Voice interpreted my wishes to him. I said, "Two Moons, I have come to hear your story of the Custer Battle, for they tell me you were a chief there. After you tell me the story, I want to take some photographs of you. I want you to signal with a blanket as the great chiefs used to do in fight."

Wolf Voice made this known to him, delivering also a message from the agents, and at every pause Two Moons uttered deep-voiced notes of comprehension. "Ai," "A-ah," "Hoh,"—these sounds are commonly called "grunts," but they were low, long-drawn expulsions of breath, very expressive.

Then a long silence intervened. The old man mused. It required time to go from the silence of the hot valley, the shadow of his little cabin, and the wire fence of his pasture, back to the days of his youth. When he began to speak, it was with great deliberation. His face became each moment graver and his eyes more introspective.

"Two Moons does not like to talk about the days of fighting, but since you are to make a book, and the agent says you are a friend to Grinnell (George B. Grinnell, whom the Cheyennes, Blackfeet, and Gross Ventres love and honor), I will tell you about it— the truth. It is now a long time ago, and my words do not come quickly.

"That spring [1876] I was camped on Powder River with fifty lodges of my people—Cheyennes. The place is near what is now Fort McKinney. One morning soldiers charged my camp. They were in command of Three Fingers [Col. Ranald S. MacKenzie]. We were surprised and scattered, leaving our ponies. The soldiers ran all our horses off. That night the soldiers slept, leaving the horses [on] one side; so we crept up and stole them back again, and then we went away.[2]

"We travelled far, and one day we met a big camp of Sioux, and had a good time, plenty of grass, plenty game, good water. Crazy Horse was head chief of the camp. Sitting Bull was camped a little ways below, on the Little Missouri River.[3]

---

[2]Fort McKinney was constructed in 1876, near the present site of Buffalo, Wyoming, in accordance with new demands for troops and military posts following the humiliating defeat at the Little Bighorn.

[3]Crazy Horse was an Oglala Lakota who was born near Bear Butte, South Dakota, in 1840. He was one of the most respected individuals among the warlike Sioux, his name representing the epitome of Indian resistance to white encroachment. While resisting arrest, he was bayonetted by Pvt. William Gentles at Camp Robinson, Nebraska, on September 5, 1877, and died the same day. For a stirring biography of this individual, see Mari Sandoz, *Crazy Horse: The Strange Man of the Oglalas* (Lincoln, 1961); and also Richard G. Hardorff, *The Oglala Lakota Crazy Horse: A Preliminary Genealogical Study and an Annotated Listing of Primary Sources* (Mattituck, 1985).

Sitting Bull was a ranked member of the Strong Heart Society and the spiritual leader of the Hunkpapa Lakotas. He was born on the Grand River near the present town of Bullhead, South Dakota, in 1831, near which location he was slain while resisting arrest on December 15, 1890. For his biography, see Stanley Vestal, *Sitting Bull, Champion of the Sioux*, By request of his direct descendants, Sitting Bull's remains were exhumed from the Fort Yates Cemetery, North Dakota, on April 8, 1953, and reinterred that same day near Mobridge, South Dakota. This exhumation released an angry exchange of charges and counter charges between both states regarding the jurisdiction over the remains and the legality of the transfer across state lines, its feud eventually resolved by the federal authorities. For an entertaining volume on this matter, see Robb De Wall, *The Saga of Sitting Bull's Bones* (Crazy Horse, 1984).

"Crazy Horse said to me, 'I'm glad you are come [sic]. We are going to fight the white man again.' The camp was already full of wounded men, women, and children. I said to Crazy Horse, 'All right. I am ready to fight. I have fought already. My people have been killed, my horses stolen; I am satisfied to fight."

Here the old man paused a moment, and his face took on a lofty and somber expression.

"I believed at the time the Great Spirits had made Sioux, [and] put them there," he drew a circle to the right—"and white men and Cheyennes here,"—indicating two places to the left—"expecting them to fight. The Great Spirits, I thought, liked to see the fight; it was to them all the same like playing. So I thought then about fighting." As he said this, he made me feel for one moment the power of a sardonic god whose drama was the wars of men.

"About May, when the grass was tall and the horses strong, we broke camp and started across the country to the mouth of the Tongue River. Then Sitting Bull and Crazy Horse and all went up the Rosebud. There we had a big fight with General [George] Crook and whipped him. Many soldiers were killed—few Indians. It was a great fight, [with] much smoke and dust.[4]

"From there we all went over the divide, and camped in the valley of the Little Horn. Everybody thought, 'Now we are out of the white man's country. He can live there, we will live here.' After a few days, one morning when I was in camp north of Sitting Bull, a Sioux messenger rode up and said, 'Let everybody paint up, cook, and get ready for a big dance.'

---

[4]The U.S. Military casualties consisted of ten killed, including a young boy of the Shoshone auxiliary contingent. The loss of the opposing Indian force consisted of four Lakotas and one Cheyenne. However, the exaggerated Indian loss reported by the Military was thirteen killed, including a disabled Lakota who, blinded by a gunshot, was killed and mutilated by Crow Indians the following day. See Vaughn, *With Crook on the Rosebud*, 156, 214; and also the White Bull Interview, Campbell Collection..

"Cheyennes then went to work to cook, cut up tobacco, and get ready. We all thought to dance all day. We were glad to think we were far away from the white man.

"I went to water my horses at the creek, and washed them off with cool water, then took a swim myself. I came back to the camp afoot. When I got near my lodge, I looked up the Little Horn towards Sitting Bull's camp. I saw a great dust rising. It looked like a whirlwind. Soon [a] Sioux horseman came rushing into camp shouting: 'Soldiers come! Plenty white soldiers.'

"I ran into my lodge, and said to my brother-in-law, 'Get your horses; the white man is coming. Everybody run for horses.'

"Outside, far up the valley, I heard a battle cry, Hay-ay, hay-ay! I heard shooting, too, this way [clapping his hands very fast]. I couldn't see any Indians. Everybody was getting horses and saddles. After I had caught my horse, a Sioux warrior came again and said, 'Many soldiers are coming.' Then he said to the women, 'Get out of the way, we are going to have a hard fight.' I said, 'All right, I am ready.'

"I got on my horse and rode out into my camp. I called out to the people all running about: 'I am Two Moons, your chief. Don't run away. Stay here and fight. You must stay and fight the white soldiers. I shall stay even if I am to be killed.'

"I rode swiftly toward Sitting Bull's camp. There I saw white soldiers fighting in a line [Reno's men]. Indians covered the flat. They began to drive the soldiers [and] all was mixed up—Sioux, then soldiers, then more Sioux, and all shooting. The air was full of smoke and dust. I saw the soldiers fall back and drop into the riverbed like buffalo fleeing. They had no time to look for a crossing. The Sioux chased them up the hill, where they met more soldiers in wagons,[5]

---

[5]Two Moons is in error because the wagons of the Dakota Column were left behind at

and then messengers came saying more soldiers were going to kill the women, and the Sioux turned back. Chief Gall was there fighting.[6] Crazy Horse also.

"I then rode toward my camp and stopped squaws from carrying off lodges. While I was sitting on my horse I saw flags come up over the hill to the east like that (he raised his fingertips). Then the soldiers rose all at once, all on horses, like this (he put his fingers behind each other to indicate that Custer appeared marching in columns of fours). They formed into three branches with a little ways between. Then a bugle sounded, and they all got off [their] horses, and some soldiers led the horses back over the hill.

"Then the Sioux rode up the ridge on all sides, riding very fast. The Cheyennes went up the left way. The shooting was quick, quick. Pop—pop—pop, very fast. Some of the white soldiers were down on their knees, some standing. Officers all in front. The smoke was like a great cloud, and everywhere the Sioux went, the dust rose like smoke. We circled all around them—swirling like water round a stone. We shoot, we ride fast, we shoot again. Soldiers drop, and horses fall on them. Soldiers in line drop, but one man rides up and down the line—all the time shouting. He rode a sorrel horse with white face and white forelegs. I don't know who he was. He was a brave man.[7]

---

the supply depot at the mouth of the Powder River. The logistical system of the Seventh Cavalry consisted of a pack train of some 175 mules. See Richard G. Hardorff, "Packs, Packers, and Pack Details: Logistics and Custer's Pack Train," in Gregory T.W. Urwin and Roberta E. Fagan, eds., *Custer and His Times, Book Three* (Conway, AR, 1987) 225-48.

[6]Gall, also known as Man Who Goes in the Middle, was born in a Hunkpapa Lakota camp on the Grand River, South Dakota, in 1840. Throughout his nonreservation life he proved himself a fierce opponent to the white aggressors. He surrendered to the Military in 1880, and later became a justice of the Indian Police Court at Standing Rock Agency. Gall passed away in 1893, and was buried at Wakpala, South Dakota. See Lewis F. Crawford; *Rekindling Camp Fires: The Exploits of Ben Arnold* (Bismarck, 1926), 166-68; Usher L. Burdick. *David F. Barry's Indian Notes on the Custer Battle* (Baltimore, 1949), 33, 35.

[7]The Minneconjou, Red Horse, may have spoken of this same individual whose gallant

"Indians keep swirling round and round, and the soldiers killed only a few. Many soldiers fell. At last all horses [were] killed but five. Once in a while some man would break out and run toward the river, but he would fall. At last about a hundred men and five horsemen stood on the hill, all bunched together. All along the bugler kept blowing his commands. He was very brave too. Then a chief was killed. I hear it was Long Hair [Custer], I don't know; and then the five horsemen and the bunch of men, may be so forty, started toward the river. The man on the sorrel horse led them, shouting all the time. (This man's identity is in dispute. He was apparently a scout.) He wore a buckskin shirt, and had long black hair and mustache. He fought hard with a big knife. His men were all covered with white dust.[8] I couldn't tell whether they were officers or not. One man all alone ran far down toward the river, then round up over the hill. I thought he was going to escape, but a Sioux fired and hit him in the head. He was the last man. He wore braids on his arms [a non-commissioned officer].[9]

"All the soldiers were now killed, and the bodies were stripped. After that no one could tell which [ones] were officers. The bodies were left where they fell. We had no dance that night. We were sorrowful.

"Next day four Sioux chiefs and two Cheyennes and I,

---

conduct left a lasting impression on the Indians; however, the identity of this soldier is not known. See Graham, *The Custer Myth*, 57-60, 61.

On June 25, Custer rode Vic, abbreviated from *victory*, a sorrel horse with four white feet and a blaze in the face. See John Burkman, Custer's orderly, to Elizabeth Custer, 2/3/1911, Elizabeth B. Custer Collection, Roll 3, Custer Battlefield National Monument; and also Graham, *The Custer Myth*, 345.

[8]According to the Lakota, Lone Elk, only nine of these soldiers were mounted, while the Oglala, He Dog, revealed that the dismounted soldiers ran to Deep Ravine, while those who were mounted tried to escape toward Calhoun Ridge. See Hardorff, *Markers*, 59; and also Hammer, *Custer in '76*, 207.

Two Moons, went upon the battlefield to count the dead. One man carried a little bundle of sticks. When we came to dead men, we took a little stick and gave it to another man, so we counted the dead. There were 388.[10] There were thirty-nine Sioux and seven Cheyennes killed, and about a hundred wounded.[11]

"Some white soldiers were cut with knives, to make sure they were dead; and the war women had mangled some. Most of them were left just where they fell. We came to the man with [the] big mustache; he lay down the hill towards the river. (Custer fell higher up on the ridge.) The Indians did not take his buckskin shirt. The Sioux said, 'That is a big chief. That is Long Hair.' I don't know. I had never seen him. The man on the white-faced horse was the bravest man.

"That day as the sun was getting low our young men came up the Little Horn riding hard. Many white soldiers were coming in a big boat, and when we looked we could see the smoke rising.[12] I called my people together, and we hurried up the Little Horn, into Rotten Grass Valley. We camped there three days, and then rode swiftly back over our old trail to the east. Sitting Bull went back into the Rosebud and

---

[9]After the battle, the bodies of two non-commissioned officers were found at isolated sites south of Calhoun Ridge, suggesting that one of these two men was the individual spoken of by Two Moons. Sgt. James Butler of L Company was found on the heights west of Luce Ridge, his mutilated body lying amidst numerous cartridge casings, which attested to his courage. Corp. John Foley of C Troop managed to ride as far as Medicine Tail Ford where luck ran out on him and where he committed suicide. See Hardorff, *Markers*, 28-30.

[10]Two Moons is mistaken, because the U.S. Military loss amounted to fifteen officers, 237 enlistees, eight civilians, and three U.S. Indian Scouts. See Hardorff, *Custer Battle Casualties*, 93, 123.

[11]For a comprehensive study of the names of the slain Indians, the circumstances of their deaths, and the location of their kill sites, see Hardorff, *Hokahey! A Good Day to Die!*.

[12]This was the steamer *Far West* which navigated the Big Horn River on June 26, and which lost its bearings while searching for the mouth of the Little Bighorn. See Joseph Mills Hanson, *The Conquest of the Missouri* (New York: 1946), 271-72.

down the Yellowstone, and away to the north. I did not see him again." (This was a wonderful retreat.)

The old man paused and filled his pipe. His story was done. His mind came back to his poor people on the barren land where the rain seldom falls.

"That was a long time ago. I am now old and my mind has changed. I would rather see my people living in houses and singing and dancing. You have talked with me about fighting, and I have told you of the time long ago. All that is past. I think of these things now: First, that our reservation shall be fenced and the white settlers kept out and our young men kept in. Then there will be no trouble. Second, I want to see my people raising cattle and making butter. Last, I want to see my people going to school to learn the white man's way. That is all."

There was something placid and powerful in the lines of the chief's broad brow, and his gestures were dramatic and noble in sweep. His extended arms, his musing eyes, his deep voice combined to express a meditative solemnity profoundly impressive. There was no anger in his voice, and no reminiscent ferocity. All that was strong and fine and distinctive in the Cheyenne character came out in the old man's talk. He seemed the leader and the thoughtful man he really is—patient under injustice, courteous even to his enemies.

J.M. Thralls' Interview with Two Moons

INTRODUCTION

The following interview with Two Moons was taken from an article by J.M. Thralls in the Kansas State Historical Society Collections, Volume XVI, which contained the contributions submitted from 1923 to 1925. Thralls was a pioneer of the Southwest. He had lived on the Kansas frontier since the 1860s and at one time had served as the mayor of the town of Wellington in Kansas.

The article was submitted by Thralls in 1924. The contents reflect his reminiscences of long ago because Thralls was unaware of Two Moons' death in 1917. The actual interview date is not given, but I believe that it may have taken place in 1901 for reasons explained in the introduction to the *Harness Gazette* interview, which follows hereafter. There exist some similarities between Thralls' interview and the one recorded by the *Gazette*, suggesting the same year of origin. It is quite possible, therefore, that Thralls referred to the *Gazette* when he wrote that among the five whites present during the interview, one was "a writer of some magazine."

If the interview date of 1901 is indeed correct, the superintendent spoken of by Thralls was A.N. Grover who was appointed in 1893 and who served in that capacity until April 1906. The following is a copy of the original article, except that I have deleted

Thralls' opinions of the battle. In addition, I have corrected errors in spelling and grammar and have provided punctuation when needed.

J.M. THRALLS' INTERVIEW
Custer Battlefield, Montana, 1901

... The history of the West contains no more thrilling episode than the defeat of General Custer at the hands of the Sioux Indian, Chief Sitting Bull, and other confederate tribes, among whom was the band of Two Moons, [a] Northern Cheyenne chief, with fifty lodges.

The battleground is fenced in, in one tract, by a board fence. The tract, as I remember it, is about one mile and a half long by one-half to three-quarters of a mile wide. Inside this enclosure is the superintendent's residence. Soon after my arrival at the latter place, early in the morning, Two Moons, the Cheyenne chief, and four of his men who were with him in the fight, came together with about fifteen young agency Indians. Besides these, there were a white man and his wife, the superintendent, a writer of some magazine, and myself. The last five were the only whites present.[1]

---

[1] General Orders No. 7, Headquarters of the Army, established Custer's battlefield as a National Cemetery of the fourth class as of August 1, 1879. In 1946, it was renamed Custer Battlefield National Monument when stewardship of the site was transferred to the Department of Interior. Geographically, the Monument is located on the east bank of the Little Bighorn River, in Big Horn County, Montana, and its land area consists of two disconnected sites. The Custer Battlefield proper is a rectangular plot of roughly one square mile, while the Reno-Benteen area, located five miles farther south along the river, consists of a parcel of some 162 acres. Efforts are currently under way to acquire the historically significant land parcels adjacent to the Monument through private donations. The first custodian was James A. Campbell who was housed at nearby Fort Custer and who served from 1880 to 1892. In 1893, A.N. Grover was appointed as superintendent, serving in this capacity until April 1906. See Hardorff, *Custer Battle Casualties,* 69; Don Rickey, Jr., "Myth to Monument: The Establishment of Custer Battlefield National Monument," *Journal of the West* (April 1968), 203-04; Capt. Charles Walcut to Walter Camp, 5/29/1909, Walter Camp Collection, Brigham Young University Library.

We went out upon the field near where the big monument now stands and gathered around Two Moons and his four men and his interpreter, a young Cheyenne.[2] From where we stood we could see the whole of the battlefield over which General Custer fought. We could also see the top of the timber where Reno commenced his fight—about three miles southeast of the monument. We began at once asking Two Moons all kinds of questions about the battle, how and where the soldiers were located on the battlefield. He would described the locations by the color of their horses: "The soldiers with the white horse over there, red horse over there, black horse over there," indicating the direction by pointing his finger.[3] He said the first fighting commenced down the "Little Horn," meaning the Little Bighorn, with Major Reno, where he struck one end of their big camp about one mile from where Two Moons' band was camped.

He said the Indians did not know there were any soldiers near them until Major Reno's command came in contact with them. All the Indians were getting ready to go and fight Reno, when Custer's command came into sight on the ridge northeast of where the Indians were in camp. As soon as it was seen how large, or how small, Custer's command was, orders were given by the chiefs to all of the old warriors in front of Reno to go and fight Custer, leaving the young warriors to hold Reno.

He said the first soldiers killed were sixteen horse-holders. Perhaps these were [Capt. Myles] Keogh's and [Lt. James]

---

[2]This monument, cut in three sections, formed a truncated stone pyramid some 11½ ft. high, 6 ft. wide at the base and 3½ ft. at the top. Weighing some 38,547 pounds, its placement was completed on July 30, 1881, by Lt. Charles F. Roe, its location being six feet in the rear of Custer's kill site. See Hardorff, *Custer Battle Casualties*, 70-71.

[3]Two Moons is mistaken as none of Custer's five companies rode black horses. Black horses were assigned to D Troop of Capt. Benteen's battalion. See Graham, *The Custer Myth*, 346.

Calhoun's men, one mile and a half east of the monument.[4] This was followed by the complete annihilation of these two companies by the Sioux warriors commanded by Chiefs Gall and Rain in the Face.[5] Chief Two Moons and his band of Cheyennes, consisting, he said, of fifty lodges, went down the river and around west and northwest of what was left of Custer's command. He showed where they dismounted and crawled up to the top of the ridge overlooking a draw that now contains ninety-two soldier monuments in about a quarter of a mile.[6] He said, "When Injins come here, soldiers [were] down below. Injins kill'em, kill'em, kill'em," pointing out the location of Indians and soldiers. They then turned their attention to General Custer and the few who had gathered around him.

General Custer fell only a few steps from the site of the monument, at the high point of the hill, the spot where he fell being marked by a cross.[7] He told us of nineteen men who

---

[4]These horse holders were killed on the north slope of Calhoun Ridge, because it was here that the Brule, Hollow Horn Bear, observed mounted soldiers who were holding the horses for those who were deployed on foot. This location is confirmed by the Hunkpapa, Moving Robe Woman, who noticed these horse holders immediately after she crossed the river at Medicine Tail Ford. See Hardorff, *Lakota Recollections*, 95, 182.

[5]Born near the forks of the Cheyenne River in 1836, Rain in the Face was one of two Hunkpapa sons born out of his father's second marriage. Rain's younger brother was Shave Head, a sergeant in the Standing Rock Indian police who was killed in the line of duty during the arrest of Sitting Bull in 1890. In 1873, Rain was implicated in the killing of two civilians along the Yellowstone.

He was arrested in 1875 and imprisoned at Fort Lincoln, from where he escaped the same year, swearing vengeance on the Custers. There are conflicting reports whether Rain actually participated in the Custer Battle; however, the extreme mutilation of Tom Custer's body gave rise to the immediate speculation about Rain's involvement. His reputation as Custer's slayer was firmly cemented by the writings of Elizabeth Custer and Longfellow's poem, "The Revenge of Rain in the Face." Rain died at Standing Rock Agency in 1905. See Charles H. Eastman, "Rain-in-the-Face," *The Outlook* (October 27, 1906), 507; James McLaughlin, *My Friend the Indian* (Seattle, 1970), 178.

[6]Reference is made to the draw which runs on the north side of Custer Ridge, and where some ninety markers stretch northwestward from Calhoun Hill for about half a mile.

broke away from the Custer group, evidently after General Custer's death, under command of a brave officer. He pointed to the seventeen monuments that showed the circle in which they ran.[8] He said two men came near getting away. One stone marked the grave of one who had fallen the farthest northeast. The other, he said, got away a mile before he was killed.[9] The authorities say the body was never found. That was partly explained by the fact that some bones of men from which the dogs had eaten the flesh were found in the Indian's camp.

We asked him what became of the soldiers' horses during the fight. Waving both arms, he said, "Soldiers horses ran all over. Squaws ketch'em and take 'em to Little Horn about one mile south." In answer to when they scalped and mutilated the bodies, he said the squaws followed up and scalped the soldiers. We asked him how many Indians were killed. He said, "Heap Injins killed, heap Injins killed." We asked how many Indians in the fight. He said he did not know, "Most Sioux, heap lodges," and named a few other tribes that I do not recollect. Of Cheyennes he had fifty lodges, pointing out about five miles along the river where they all were camped.

We talked about two hours and a half with him, or rather asked him questions for about that long. At some questions which we asked him, he would turn to his four men who were in the fight with him and talked for two or three minutes before answering us. They would look and point over the

---

[7]Being located some fifty feet from the monument, the present marker for Gen. Custer does *not* identify his kill site, but rather it marks the *burial* site at the base of the knoll where he and his brother, Tom, were interred. See Hardorff, *Markers*, 5, 7.

[8]This interview fails to identify the location of these nineteen markers. However, I assume that these stones stood somewhere near Deep Ravine, based on what Two Moons told Hamlin Garland about this final phase of the battle.

[9]The attempted escapes were witnessed by Big Beaver and Young Two Moons whose recollections follow hereafter.

field as though refreshing their memories. He claimed this was the first time he had ever been on the battlefield since the fight. He said they heard more soldiers were coming, so they left next day after the fight. As we were talking, we would ask the superintendent of the grounds if his story was correct as he understood it. He would answer that it was about as he had heard it.

Two Moons gave us the impression that he was telling the truth as near as he recollected. He said he did not know how old he was then, but he was thirty-seven [34] at the time of the fight. As that was forty-eight years ago, he would now (1924) be eighty-five [82] years old. At the time I saw him, he was very straight, about six feet tall, and had a set of teeth that would be the envy of any one. He was dressed in a pair of old canton flannel pants, a light calico shirt, a pair of moccasins, and wore a light blanket over his shoulders. He had no kind of ornaments on his person.

In all of our talk with him he never smiled or showed exultant feeling over their victory, nor anger in his voice. At the end of our questioning he told his interpreter to tell us "That is all I know." After this I asked him what kind of gun he used in the fight. He answered direct: "Soldier gun; one of Crook's guns. We whipped Crook eight days before. Killed heap soldiers and got gun." He could talk a little English [and] would answer short questions direct without the interpreter. Said they got "heap soldier cartridges off all soldiers' saddles"(meaning out of the saddlebag pockets). He said he did not expect any soldiers. Asked why they did not all go and finish Reno, he said, "Heap warriors did go; heap stayed in camp to protect women and children and ponies." They had a big war dance all night, [and] said [that] young warriors rode all over the battlefield and killed wounded soldiers and gathered up soldier guns. He said they did not find many cartridges on soldiers.

In giving the location of the Indians in the battle, Chief Two Moons mentioned Sitting Bull and Chiefs Gall and Crazy Horse often. In looking over the field and location of the soldiers and the Indians, one is impressed with the idea that the Indians outmaneuvered the General at all points, caught his command broken up in small detachments, when they massed their warriors against the separate detachments and killed them in detail...

It was a fearful price that was paid on the day of the Custer battle for what was apparently a mismanaged campaign—the massacre of the whole of Custer's command. But why call it a massacre any more than if our army were fighting an enemy other than Indians? The battle was fought in an open field, slightly hilly, covered with short sagebrush. The Indians advanced out from their camp and met General Custer's command on the ridge, outnumbering the soldiers perhaps eight or ten to one, outgeneralling our officers until they ran out of ammunition, and the rest were shot down like targets.

The Harness Gazette Interview with Two Moons

INTRODUCTION

The following interview with Two Moons was taken from a clipping of the June 1908 issue of the *Harness Gazette,* a monthly magazine first published in 1882. Unfortunately, the identity of the story writer is not revealed, and there exists uncertainty about the date when the interview took place. In view of the deadlines kept by magazine editors, it seems more likely that the interview was held in 1907, instead of 1908.

However, there is some evidence which suggests that the interview may have taken place much earlier than 1907. The *Harness Gazette* writer mentions that Two Moons' visit to the battlefield was the first since 1876. If this statement is correct, then the year of revisitation was 1901 because the caption to a photograph taken by Laton A. Huffman of Two Moons on Custer Hill identifies the date as the twenty-fifth anniversary of the Custer Battle.

Based on the photographic evidence provided by Huffman, I am inclined to believe that the *Harness Gazette* interview took place in 1901. However, for some unexplained reason, the article was not published until 1908. The following is a copy of the original, except that I have corrected errors in spelling and grammar and have provided paragraphing when needed.

THE HARNESS GAZETTE INTERVIEW
Custer Battlefield, Montana, 1901

The first time I saw Chief Two Moons he was pointed out to me in a dance tent. Ragged and unkempt, and showing the poverty that is breaking the heart of his great tribe, Two Moons sat unmoved while the tom-toms were sounding and the Crows and the Cheyennes were mingling in the Owl Dance. Around him were grouped a few Cheyenne braves, veterans of many a hard battle with white soldiers. All were ragged and poverty-stricken in appearance, like their leader, but proud and reserved, they sat apart from the festivities. Like most of the Cheyennes, the retainers of Two Moons were small in stature, their chieftain towering above them like a giant, yet our soldiers unite in declaring that these little Indians are like the Japanese—veritable demons in playing the fighting game and the bravest of all the plains tribes.

I called on Two Moons, finding him in a ragged tent in the part of the campground preempted by the Cheyennes. A handshake all around, a few pulls at the long pipe that was being circulated, and under the magic of the sweet smelling kinnikinnick, Two Moons' heart was opened and his tongue was loosened.

In answer to a question he gave me the briefest and most significant story of the Custer fight.

"Big fight," said Two Moons, who talks little English and who is under a heavy handicap in the absence of an interpreter. "Lots of Indians. Get around soldiers—so. Pretty soon, all gone—so."

To illustrate his description he had formed a circle with his hands, and then he passed one hand over the other to demonstrate how rapidly the fatal circle about Custer was closed.

A little later, with the interpreter present, the great chieftain of the fighting Cheyennes stood on the brow of Custer Hill, the central point in one of the most awe-inspiring panoramas in the West. Two Moons is nearly blind, but when directions and locations had been pointed out to him he was living over again a scene that must be indelibly impressed on his memory. Every detail of the battlefield seemed to be stamped on his mind as freshly as on that fatal June day in 1876, when the allied tribes slaughtered every one of the men under Custer. Standing on the brow of the hill, where the white headstones stretch toward the Little Bighorn from the great granite monument, Two Moons told of the Custer battle from the standpoint of one of the principal actors. In effect his story was as follows:

"We Cheyennes were down there," pointing to the south, and thereby indicating that the Cheyenne braves must have occupied the lower part of the big camp which Custer intended to strike from the north while Reno attacked from the south. "We were not looking for the white soldiers up here. They got between us and our horses before we saw them, and our squaws' yelling told us what had happened.[1] We jumped on any horses we could get and attacked. The Sioux were attacking from the north. One bunch of soldiers had black horses, another had gray horses, and one had red (sorrel) horses.[2] The black horse men dismounted down there (pointing along the ridge toward the place where Keogh and and his men made their last stand). We killed lots

---

[1]Several small pony herds were guarded by boys on the flats east of the river near Medicine Tail Ford. These boys, and the women who had fled across the river to Weir Point, saw the approach of Custer. See the statement by the Minneconjou, Standing Bear, in DeMallie, *The Sixth Grandfather*, 184-85.

[2]Custer's five troops were assigned the following colors: C Troop had light sorrels; E Troop had grays; and Troops F, I, and L had bays. See Graham, *The Custer Myth*, 346.

of them, and pretty soon they were all gone.[3] The gray horse men fell back along the ridge. (Evidently this was the group with Custer, who fell near the end of the ridge). Pretty soon they were all gone, too. The red horse men were the last to be killed.[4] They had dismounted on the other side of the ridge (pointing to where the ridge slopes to the north from the monument). Some of them tried to get away by running toward the river, but we killed them all. One got far off, but we got him, too." (This would explain the finding of bodies far down the slope toward the position of the camp in the Little Bighorn bottoms. Some military experts have maintained that these were skirmishers, thrown out ahead of the main body of Custer's men.)

As he stood on the brow of the ridge, with the Custer monument behind him and surrounded by the white headstones and the big cross that denotes where the white chief and his bodyguard fell, Two Moons made an impressive spectacle. His face was lighted with the enthusiasm of battle, and he did not seem like the same silent, reserved Indian who sat like a bronze statue in the dance tent of the Crows.

It is estimated that there were 1,000 lodges in the Indian camp along the bottoms of the Little Bighorn River. This means that there were from 4,000 to 6,000 Indians, probably half of whom were able-bodied fighting men—the best in the history of Indian warfare.[5] The Indians consisted of Sioux and Cheyennes under such leaders as Gall, Crazy

---

[3]Capt. Myles Keogh commanded I Troop which rode bay horses. However, it is perhaps possible that Two Moons mistook these horses for black ones due to their dark brown rumps and black manes and tails.

[4]The red horses identify this company as C Troop. However, it appears that the men on Custer Hill consisted of members from all five companies, because it was here that fourteen men of F Troop were found and where the Gray Horse Troop covered the retreat of the others. See Hammer, *Custer in '76*, 139.

Horse, Rain in the Face, and Two Moons. Crazy Horse and his Sioux were with the Cheyennes. Every brave in this great camp was a veteran, as all the faint-hearts in both tribes had been left on the reservations, content to draw their rations and abide by the peace treaty. The allied fighters represented the determined spirits among the plains tribes—men who preferred the hardships and dangers of the warpath to a life of ease under the white man's dominion.

Gen. Custer had divided his regiment into three detachments, two of them, under Reno and Benteen, to attack from the south and west, while Custer, with Troops C, E, F, I and L, swept around to the east and north and surprised the Indians at the rear of the camp.[6]

Reno's desperate fight is well known. He found himself confronted by a large and determined body of savage fighters, and was beaten back to the bluffs, where he remained, not daring to change his position for fear of annihilation. Only the fact that he was joined by Benteen saved him from Custer's fate. Reno heard the firing that denoted Custer's engagement, and has been criticized for not going to the aid of his commander. But a person who looks over the Custer

---

[5]These estimates are well in line with later studies. See, for example, Gray, *Centennial Campaign*, 357, in which he deduced the total Indian population at 1000 lodges, containing 7120 persons, including 1780 adult males; and also Marshall, "How Many Indians Were There?," 218, who estimated a ceiling of 795 lodges and a corresponding population of 5056 people.

[6]No such strategy was ever communicated to the surviving battalion commanders. Benteen was ordered to the south some thirteen miles east of the river, to commence a reconnaissance and to engage in a holding action if any Indians were encountered. Reno's battalion was dispatched some four miles east of the river with nearly similar orders, that is, he was to overtake and commence a holding action with a band of fleeing Indians; and it was not until Custer reached Reno Hill that he beheld the sight of an immense Indian village which was still standing in the valley below. It was probably at this location that Custer formulated his ill-fated strategy which allowed the Indians the advantage to separately engage and defeat two of his three uncoordinated combat forces.

Battlefield and hears from the Indians how advantageously the red men were situated, and how eager they were for battle, cannot see where any censure of Reno is justified in this particular. His men would have been wiped out had they tried to march over the barren hills to Custer's aid, as the plains were fairly alive with hostile Indians seeking more of the divided white forces to slay.

From Two Moons' account of the battle it is evident that the Cheyennes and the Sioux under Crazy Horse must have engaged Keogh (the troop with the black horses) at the opening of the battle.

Then the rest of the troops, scattered along the ridge as the chieftain described, met their fate. Keogh and his men were found as they had fallen. There is a little cluster of white headstones about the cross that shows where Keogh fell. From this cluster toward the monument on top of the ridge, extends a long, straight line of headstones. This shows that Keogh's men fell while in line of battle.

Myles Keogh, who opposed Two Moons in this grim tragedy on the plains, was the oldest soldier in the Seventh. He had been an officer in the Papal Zouaves in early life, and had a fine record in the Civil War. Discipline was his hobby, and he and his troop must have died gloriously.[7] Keogh's

---

[7]The son of John and Margaret Blanchfield Keogh, Myles Walter Keogh was born on March 25, 1842, at Orchard House in County Carlow, Ireland. He served with distinction in the Papal Army from 1860 till 1862, when he left for New York and served as Captain, U.S. Volunteers, in the Shenandoah Valley. He saw action at South Mountain, Antietam, Mine Run and other engagements in 1863. He served on the staff of Gen. Stoneman and was captured in Georgia in July 1864, and was held for several months. In 1865, he was breveted Lt. Colonel, U.S.V. for his uniform gallantry and good conduct during the war, and was honorably mustered out after having participated in over thirty general engagements. He was commissioned Second Lieutenant, 4th Cavalry, in 1866, and was subsequently transferred to 7th Cavalry with rank of Captain. In 1867, he received the brevets of Major and Lt. Colonel for his services in the battles of Gettysburg and Dallas. Keogh died at the Little Bighorn in 1876. See Hammer, *Men with Custer* (Ft. Collins, 1972), 189. For a recent, exhaustive biography, see J. Langellier, K. Cox, and B.C. Pohanka, ed., *Myles Keogh: The Life and Legend of an Irish Dragoon in the Seventh Cavalry* (El Segundo, CA, 1991).

horse, Comanche, was found several days after the battle, badly wounded. The animal's life was saved, and he was the pet of the Seventh Regiment for many years.[8]

Since the day of the fight Two Moons had not revisited the scene of Custer's last stand until the day he told his story to the writer of this article. The old chief lives with the remnant of his tribe on a barren reservation in Montana. Their land is too poor to farm successfully; yet, under the present policy of the Government, most of their rations have been cut off. Today the Cheyennes are ragged and miserable. But the spirit within them is proud, and, in the words of a man who has lived among them, "If they had weapons and horses they would be on the warpath today." Two Moons, owing to his blindness, lost his ascendancy among the Cheyennes, but he is still the "big chief" to the few survivors of the fight on little Bighorn, and is looked upon with reverence by the few remaining veterans of this great fighting tribe.

---

[8]Contrary to popular belief, Comanche was not the property of Myles Keogh, but he instead was U.S. Government property and assigned to Pvt. John McGinnis of I Troop. Because McGinnis was convalescent at Fort Lincoln in May of 1876, Keogh requested the transfer of Comanche to his custody for use as an extra horse during the Sioux expedition. Keogh's use for Comanche becomes abundantly clear on the morning of June 25, when he chose to ride government property into battle, while entrusting his personal investment, his horse Paddy, to the protection of the pack train. As fate had it, Keogh was killed, but Comanche survived to become ironically known as Keogh's horse, never to be ridden again. Comanche died on November 7, 1891, while returning from Junction City to Fort Riley, Kansas, the cause diagnosed as overheating from being exercised too fast by his new attendant, Pvt. Winchester. See Walter Camp Manuscripts, University of Indiana Library, 78. For a biography of Comanche, see Barron Brown, *Comanche* (New York, 1973), and Elizabeth Lawrence, *His Very Silence Speaks: Comanche, The Horse Who Survived Custer's Last Stand* (Detroit, 1989).

Camp's Copy of Throssel's Interview with Two Moons

INTRODUCTION

The following interview with Two Moons was recorded by Richard Throssel in 1907, and copied some time later by Walter Camp. It may be inferred from the text that Two Moons was thirty-four at the time of the Custer Battle, which would establish 1842 as the year of his birth. This conclusion is confirmed by George B. Grinnell who noted in September 1908, that Two Moons was sixty-six years old. Consequently, Two Moons was either sixty-four or sixty-five in 1907, and not sixty-six as stated in Camp's copy, unless the interview was held in 1908.

We do not know when Walter Camp copied Throssel's interview. The records indicate that Camp visited Custer Battlefield in 1905. His next visit to Montana was in 1908, at which time he probably obtained the information. Richard Throssel was an educated Crow Indian living in Billings, Montana, and was known for his artistic talents, especially native photography. Camp's copy of the interview contains details not found in Throssel's later interview conducted in 1909, published in *Lakota Recollections*. I suspect, therefore, that some of the details may have been provided by Camp himself which, in my opinion, does not diminish its historical value.

The original text of this interview is contained in the Walter Mason Camp Collection, Brigham Young University Library. However, due to Camp's handwriting style, in addition to the fading caused by the passing of time and the fragility of the original documents, I have used the transcript prepared by Dr. Kenneth Hammer which consists of pages 606-08 in his *Custer in '76.*.

RICHARD THROSSEL'S INTERVIEW
Montana, 1907
As Told to Walter M. Camp

Two Moons' Story of [the] Custer Fight. Given to Throssel in 1907. Two Moons then sixty-six [sic] years old.

Two Moons, head chief of the Northern Cheyennes, at the age of thirty-four, was in the Crook fight on the Rosebud, June 17, 1876. After that he and some Sioux went down river thirty miles and struck westward for Sitting Bull's camp on [the] Little Bighorn. The Sioux who were with him had followed Custer as far west as Pumpkin Creek and then passed around him and went on ahead. They had their scouts out and when they arrived at the Little Bighorn informed Sitting Bull that troops were coming, and they calculated that the soldiers would arrive about June 27.[1] He went into camp at the extreme north end of the village, the Oglalas under Crazy Horse, who also came from the Crook fight, having taken position about the middle of the village.

It was decided to have a big dance in his camp before the soldiers would arrive,and preparations were made to have it come off on June 25. On that day they had taken their horses down to [the] river and watered them and were driving them

---

[1] The source of this intelligence report was probably the Brulé, Hollow Horn Bear, whose party monitored the progress of the Dakota Column near the Heart River for several days. See Hardorff, *Lakota Recollections*, 178.

out to [the]hills west of the river to let them graze,when he
noticed a heavy cloud of dust up the river and made up his
mind that soldiers had arrived. He hastily collected what
warriors he could and started in [the] direction of [the] fighting, which had already began between Gall and Reno. As
soon as he took a hand, Reno's men were forced from their
position in the timber and soon were retreating. He says that
one soldier (Lt. [Donald] McIntosh) was having trouble
with his horse, which seemed determined to go at a right
angle with the direction of the course of the fleeing troops,
instead of along with it. In this way his men easily overtook
the soldier and knocked him off his horse with a stone hammer.[2]

Seeing that the soldiers were retreating in good earnest, he
thought the Sioux could handle them, and so he drew off and
went back with his men to get them mounted and ready for
battle. He sent word to his camp that instead of a dance a
fight was on hand. In going toward his camp he had to pass
through a large population of Sioux. Here he found the old
men and women making off to the hills with the children and
otherwise preparing to desert the village and move it. He and
his leaders loudly proclaimed that they had won a victory,

---

[2]The son of James and Charlotte Robinson McIntosh, Donald McIntosh was born on
September 4, 1838, at Jasper House, near Montreal, Canada. In 1867, he received a com-
mission as a Second Lieutenant in the 7th Cavalry, and was promoted to First Lieutenant
and assigned to Troop G in 1870. McIntosh was slain on the west bank of the Little
Bighorn in 1876. During the chaos in the woods upon Reno's order to retreat, McIntosh
was unable to find his orderly who had charge of his horse. He therefore mounted a loose
horse and was among the last to leave the timber. Apparently, this horse was wounded,
while its progress was further impeded by a picket pin dragging behind on a lariat which
bothered the horse. Being of Indian descent and with pronounced facial features of his
mother's race, McIntosh was soon singled out by the hostiles and subjected to the intense
hatred shown by them to individuals who betray their own race. See Hammer, *Men with
Custer,* 151; Hammer, *Custer in '76,* 119, 132, 141.

and that there was no necessity for being alarmed for the safety of the village.

No sooner had he given these words of encouragement than it was announced that soldiers were approaching the village from the east, along Reno Creek.[3] Considerable numbers of Sioux had already gone over the river to the east side at Ford B [Medicine Tail Ford], and as Custer drew near they disappeared into ravines to the northward. Custer and his men rode up nearly to the river on their horses and were being fired upon by the Sioux posted on the west bank.[4] Here Custer stopped momentarily, and, supposing that he would cross, the Sioux began to appear on his right and rear. He says that here some soldiers were killed and were afterward dragged into the village, dismembered and burned at [the] big dance that night.[5]

Custer now turned and charged down the river at Indians who were opposing him, and his (Two Moons') warriors had by this time arrived in [a] large force with their horses. He therefore forded and followed in Custer's rear, the soldiers fighting on foot, in two wings, with the horses led between them. As Custer passed onto high ground, the Cheyennes

---

[3]Around the turn of the century, the watercourse now known as Medicine Tail Coulee was then identified as Reno Creek, and sometimes as Custer Creek. The current name use of Reno Creek applies to the winding stream bed along which Reno's battalion descended from the divide on June 25.

[4]The initial force which blocked Custer's progress at Medicine Tail Ford consisted of some ten to twenty Indians, among which were five Cheyennes. See Hammer, *Custer in '76*, 207; Stanley Vestal, *Warpath and Council Fire* (New York, 1948), 245.

[5]Although Two Moons later made a retraction, his statement is confirmed by the Hunkpapa, Little Knife, who admitted in 1879 that a soldier with stripes on his sleeves (NCO) was killed during a wild dance on the night of June 25. See the *Billings Gazette* clipping, 1926; and also the statement by Sgt. John Ryan who found human bones and parts of blue uniforms in the village. See the *Hardin Tribune*, 6/22/1923.

split and passed into ravines surrounding the soldiers. Here heavy firing was poured into the soldiers from all sides, and as successive charges were made, some part of the troops was wiped out. The soldiers with the gray horses (Troop E, Lieut. [Algernon E.] Smith) were the last to fall.[6] He did not recognize General Custer at any time during the fighting or afterward among the dead.

---

[6]This statement, although corroborated by Grinnell's informants, contradicts the earlier *Harness Gazette* article which quotes Two Moons as stating that the Red Horse Troop was the last to fall.

Joseph K. Dixon's Interview with Two Moons

INTRODUCTION

The following interview by Dr. Joseph K. Dixon with Two Moons was conducted in 1909. Of Mohawk Indian descent, Dixon first began his study of Indians in 1902. From then until his death in 1926, he was a prominent spokesman for justice and the full rights of citizenship for the Indian. As such he appeared before Congress where he also promoted the erection of a lasting Indian memorial. He was the leader of eleven Wanamaker Historical Expeditions which visited every tribe of Indians in the United States as well as Indians serving in the armed forces in World War I.

With the approval and cooperation of the Bureau of Indian Affairs, Dixon organized a Last Great Indian Council of the Plains Indians, which was to meet in the historic valley of the Little Bighorn. The purpose was to gather historical data and to make photographic records of the Indians, their manners and customs, and the country in which they lived. It was during this Last Council that Dixon interviewed Two Moons on Custer Hill.

First published in 1913, the following interview was extracted from Joseph K. Dixon's sensitive work, *The Vanishing Race,* pages 180-85.

JOSEPH K. DIXON'S INTERVIEW
Custer Battlefield, Montana, 1909

It was a September day. The hoarfrost had written the alphabet of the coming winter—there was promise of snow. With Chief Two Moons and his interpreter we climbed the dreary slopes leading to the monument and the graves of the Custer dead. Chief Two Moons took his position by the stone which reads: Brevet Major General George A. Custer, 7th U.S. Cavalry, fell here June 26th [sic], 1876." A tiny flag waved by his stone, marking the spot where the hero made his last stand. The hills all about us wore a somber hue; the sky kept marriage bonds with the scene. Cold, gray clouds hung over the ridges along which Custer rode with the daring Seventh. They draped the summits of the Big Horn Range on the far horizon in gray and purple. The prairie grass had come to the death of autumn and it, too, creaked amid the stones.

The heart beat quick at the sight of Chief Two Moons, a tall and stalwart Roman-faced Indian, standing amidst the white slabs where thirty-three years before, clad in a white shirt, red leggings, without warbonnet, he had ridden a white horse, dealing deathblows to the boys in blue, and with these deathblows ended the last great stand of the Red Man against the White Man. The battle echoes are heard again as Two Moons tells his story:

"Custer came along the ridge and across the mountains from the right of the monument. The Cheyennes and the Sioux came up the coulee from the foot of Reno Hill, and circled about. I led the Cheyennes as we came up. Custer marched up from behind the ridge on which his monument now stands, and deployed his soldiers along the entire line of the ridge. They rode over beyond where the monument stands [and] down into the valley until we could not see them.[1] The Cheyennes and Sioux came up to the right over in the valley of the Little Bighorn. Custer placed his men in groups along this ridge. The men who had dismounted along the ridge seemed to have let their horses go down the other side of the ridge.

"Those who were on the hill where the monument now stands, and where I am now standing, had gray horses and they were all in the open. The Sioux and Cheyennes came up the valley swarming like ants toward the bunch of gray horses where Long Hair stood. I led the Cheyennes up the long line of [the] ridge [running up] from the valley, blocking the soldiers, and I called to my Cheyenne brothers: 'Come on, children, do not be scared!'[2] And they came after me, yelling and firing. We broke the line of soldiers and went over the ridge. Another band of Indians and Sioux came from over beyond the ridge, and when I got over there, I got off my white horse and told my men to wait, and we loaded our guns and fired into the first troop which was very near us. At the first volley the troop at which we fired were all killed.[3]

"We kept firing along the ridge on which the troops were stationed and kept advancing. I rode my horse back along the ridge again and called upon my children to come after me.

---

[1] Two Moons' statement contradicts the generally accepted belief that Last Stand Hill was Custer's farthest point of advance. However, there exists additional evidence which suggests that units of Custer's command advanced some distance beyond this point. It is quite possible, therefore, that the kill sites of Sgt. Maj. William H. Sharrow and one other soldier mark the location of this advanced position. See, for example, White Bull's map in Hardorff, *Lakota Recollections*, 125; Stands in Timber and Liberty, *Cheyenne Memories*, 199; and Hardorff, *Markers*, 52. For an extensive treatment of this see Fox, *Archaeology, History and Custer's Last Battle*, 173-194.

[2] Two Moons' use of language in reference to the fight, his tribesmen, and his standing among them, is out of line with Cheyenne character. It is very likely, therefore, that Two Moons' recounting played on the gullibility of the interviewer. According to Wooden Leg, Two Moons filled the ears of his white audience with lies, while the Cheyennes were laughing among themselves about what he was saying. See Marquis, *Wooden Leg*, 349.

[3] This action probably occurred around Calhoun Hill and involved members of L Troop.

Many of my Cheyenne brothers were killed,[4] and I whipped up my horse and told them to come on, that this was the last day they would ever see their chief, and I again started for the bunch of gray horses on the hilltop. The Indians followed me, yelling and firing. I could not break the line at the bunch of the gray horses and I wheeled and went to the left down the valley with the line of soldiers facing me as I went, firing at me, and all my men firing at the soldiers.

"Then I rode on up the ridge to the left. I met an Indian with a big warbonnet on, and right there I saw a wounded soldier. I killed him and jumped off my horse and scalped him. The Indian I met was Black Bear, a Cheyenne.[5] I then rode down the ridge and came to a group of four dead soldiers; one of them had on a red flannel shirt, the other three had red stripes on the arm—one had three stripes [while] the other had three stripes and a sword. They all had on good clothes, and I jumped off my horse and took their clothes and their guns.

"When I turned back, I could not see anything but soldiers and Indians all mixed up together. You could hardly tell one from the other. As I rode along the ridge I found nearly all the soldiers killed. I again rode up to the ridge along which Custer's troops had been stationed. I found two or three killed and saw one running away to get on top of the high hills beyond, and we took after him and killed him.

"The whole valley was filled with smoke and the bullets flew all about us, making a noise like bees. We could hardly hear anything for the noise of the guns. When the guns were firing, [the sight] of the Sioux and Cheyennes and the sol-

---

[4]The Cheyenne dead count consisted of seven males, five of whom fell on Custer's battlefield.

[5]Black Bear, or Charcoal Bear, was a Northern Cheyenne and the keeper of the tribal Medicine Lodge and the sacred Buffalo Hat. See Marquis, *Wooden Leg,* 187.

diers—one falling one way and one falling another—together with the noise of the guns, I shall never forget. At last we saw that Custer and his men were grouped on the side of the hill, and we commenced to circle round and round, [both] the Sioux and the Cheyennes, and we all poured in on Custer and his men, firing into them until the last man was shot. We then jumped off our horses, took their guns, and scalped them.[6]

"After the fight was over, we gathered in the river bottom and cut willow sticks, [and] then some Indians were delegated to go and throw down a stick wherever they found a dead soldier, and then they were ordered to pick up the sticks again, and in this way we counted the number of dead. It was about six times we had to cut willow sticks, because we kept finding men all along the ridge. We counted four hundred eighty-eight [bodies] with our sticks along the ridge.[7] We were trying to count the dead there in the valley when General [Alfred H.] Terry came up from the other side and we fled away.

"After the battle was over, the Indians made a circle all over the ridges and around through the valley to see if they could find any more soldiers, as they were determined to kill every one. The next morning after the fight we went up behind the Reno Field and camped at Black Lodge River. We then followed Black Lodge River until we came back to the Little Bighorn again. Then we camped at the Little Bighorn, moving our camp constantly, fearing pursuit by the soldiers.

---

[6]Although some of the fighting around Calhoun Hill was conducted by Indians on horseback, the assault on Custer Hill was not. See, for example, the account by Big Beaver hereafter.

[7]Two Moons count does not make any sense. Although he told Garland that 388 whites had been killed, this number had now swollen to 488, while in actuality the dead count was only 263, of which 212 were on Custer's battlefield. See Hardorff, *Custer Battle Casualties*, 123.

"Before the Custer fight, we went over on the Tongue River and found a camp of soldiers. We rushed upon them and took all their horses away, and the soldiers ran into the brush. We knew there would be other soldiers after us; we knew about where they were, and we felt they would pursue us. At Powder River the soldiers attacked our camp and destroyed everything, and that made us mad. When the soldiers came after us, on the day of the Custer fight, we were ready to kill them all. The soldiers were after us all the time, and we had to fight."

The lonely stretches of the prairie, the lonelier graves, the pathetic remnant of Red Men—victors on this field—the hollow silence of these dreary slopes, the imperishable valor of two hundred seventy-seven men who laid their lives on a blood-red altar, until the one lone figure of the great captain lifted his unavailing sword against a howling horde of savage warriors— glittering for a moment in the June sunlight, then falling to the earth baptized with blood—is the solemn picture to forever hang in the nation's gallery of battles.

[Addendum by Dixon:] Chief Two Moons wears about his neck an immense cluster of bear claws. His arms are also encircled with this same insignia of distinction. Although he has reached the age of nearly threescore years and ten, his frame is massive and his posture, when standing, typifies the forest oak. It takes no conjuring of the imagination to picture this stalwart leader of the Cheyennes against Custer on that fateful June day, as suffering no loss in comparison with the great generals who led the Roman eagles to victory. Two Moons is now nearly blind, he carries his coup stick, covered with a wolf skin, both as a guide for his footsteps and a badge of honour. There is not a tinge of gray in the ample folds of his hair, and his voice is resonant and strong.

Miscellaneous Interviews

LONG FOREHEAD STANDS SECOND FROM LEFT IN THIS PHOTOGRAPH
taken by D.L. Gill in Washington, D.C., in March 1913.
Better known to whites as Willis Rowland, he acted as
interpreter for the Northern Cheyenne delegation.
Individuals identified, left to right are: (seated) Young Little
Wolf and Two Moons; (standing) Wooden Leg, Willis Rowland,
Blue Hawk, Shoulder Blade, and Black Wolf.
Photo courtesy of Smithsonian Institution, National Anthropological Archives.

The Long Forehead Interview

INTRODUCTION

Better known to the whites as Willis Rowland, Long Forehead and his father, William Young Rowland, are prominently mentioned in scholarly works relating to the Northern Cheyenne Indians. For that reason, a biographical outline of the Rowland family may benefit the reader in evaluating the interview which follows.

Born in 1830, William Young Rowland was a Kentucky native and a member of Stanbury's surveying expedition to Great Salt Lake in 1849. The following year, William settled on Plum Creek near Denver where he operated a ranch. He maintained friendly ties with the neighboring Cheyennes, and in the same year he married a daughter of Frog, a renowned chief. However, during a quarrel with his wife's three brothers, William shot one of them, while in turn he received a blow to the head with a club which broke his cranium. His ranch was burned to the ground and his wife fled with her three brothers, thinking he had died. Miraculously, William survived the trauma of his wound, but for the rest of his life he carried a silver disk implanted in his skull to cover the hole.

After regaining his strength, William drifted north and eventually found his wife in a Cheyenne camp along the Platte in 1851. Known to the Cheyennes as Long Knife, William was once again accepted by them. He was living with the tribe near Fort Laramie in 1854, and even joined them in their hereditary war against the

Pawnees a few years later. When the Cheyennes vacated the Platte Valley in the middle 1860s, William and his family stayed at Fort Laramie where he was employed as post interpreter. Eventually, he moved to Fort Robinson in northwestern Nebraska to accept a similar position, and in 1873 he accompanied the Cheyenne delegation to Washington as their interpreter.

During the Sioux War of 1876, William was in charge of a small auxiliary force of Cheyenne Indian Scouts under Lt. William P. Clark, among whom were Hard Robe, Little Fish, and Roan Bear. These were his wife's brothers, one of whom he had wounded. However, the family quarrel had been settled long ago, and together they fought Dull Knife's Cheyennes. After the Sioux War, William remained at Fort Robinson where he rendered his services during the tragic outbreak of the imprisoned Cheyennes in 1879.

William Rowland's services as an interpreter may have spanned some thirty years, ending with the disbandment of Lt. Casey's Cheyenne Indian Scouts at Fort Keogh in 1895. Very little is known about William's later life. Records reveal that he operated a trading post near the confluence of the Rosebud and the Muddy, some six miles below Lame Deer, where he lived with his aged parents and a younger brother. William passed away in 1907. George Grinnell, who was well acquainted with him, described William as an excellent scout and interpreter, and "a fine type of the old-time prairie man—resourceful, without fear, and a good companion to travel with through hostile country."

William Rowland had a large family. It consisted of eight sons—William, James, Willis, Benjamin, Zachary, Franklin, Edward, and Clay—and two daughters, named Alice and Mary. Of all these children, only Willis, Zachary and Mary were still living in 1920.

William's oldest son was William Young Rowland, Jr. Like his father, he, too, was employed by the military. The evidence, however, is contradictory as to the nature of his services. It appears that he may have been a member of the Indian Police stationed at the Tongue River Reservation. Born about 1857, William, Jr., was involved in the Head Chief incident of 1890, which resulted in the deaths of two young Cheyennes. Since William, Jr., was half Cheyenne, rumors floated around that he had violated Cheyenne tribal law which governed homicide. Two years later, William, Jr., suddenly died from causes unknown. But in the small Cheyenne community it was whispered that someone had placed a curse on him.

With the exception of Willis Rowland, very little data is available on the other children of William Young Rowland. His second son was named James Oscar. He was employed as an interpreter at Ft. Robinson where he assisted his father during the Cheyenne Outbreak in 1879. Of William's two daughters, the records indicate that Alice, the older one, married Charles Parker, a soldier stationed at Ft. Keogh. The youngest daughter, Mary, later married Edward Powell. We also know that William's fifth son was named Zachary. The latter's image was captured on a photograph taken in 1892 by Laton A. Huffman of Lt. Casey's Cheyenne Indian Scouts, in which Zachary had enlisted. Zachary's older brother, Willis, served in this same company as first sergeant.

Willis Thompson Rowland was William Young Rowland's third son and was born along the Platte River in 1862. Throughout his life he stayed with his mother's people, the Cheyennes, who accepted and knew him as Long Forehead, the grandson of Frog. Willis later married Helen, the youngest daughter of the respected Cheyenne, Elk River. This union resulted in a family of six sons—Thomas, Richard, William, George, Rhody, and Edward—and one daughter, Blanche.

Willis Thompson Rowland served as an interpreter nearly all of his life. Skilled in the use of the difficult Cheyenne language, he was also often asked to interpret Cheyenne culture. It is no surprise, therefore, that his service record includes U.S. Military personnel, historians, sociologists, ethnologists, and many others who were genuinely interested in the Cheyennes. Throughout his entire life, Willis walked the difficult road between two cultures. He did so in an outstanding manner, and much of what we know of the Tongue River Cheyennes, we owe to the translations of this gentle and sensitive man. His expertise was eagerly sought by such notables as George B. Grinnell, Thomas B. Marquis, George E. Hyde, Walter Camp, Stanley Vestal, and E. Adamson Hoebel. Perhaps the keenest evaluation of Willis Rowland's skills was given by Hoebel who wrote that Willis' interpretations were slow spoken, solid, and careful; that he worked like a craftsman; that his vocabulary was apt, and the use of it careful; and that his rendering of Cheyenne came in painstaking detail.

The following transcript is a verbatim copy of a special dispatch forwarded from Lame Deer to the *Billings* (Montana) *Gazette*, appearing in the issue of May 26, 1927. The transcript was made from a clipping housed in the Billings Clipping File, Billings Public Library.

THE LONG FOREHEAD INTERVIEW
Lame Deer, Montana, 1927

No Indian knows how General Custer died at the battle of the Little Bighorn as there was so much smoke and dust in the air that the soldiers could hardly be seen and the Indians could not make out what was going on except that they were firing into the troop of soldiers, according to statements made by Cheyenne Indians who actually took part in the fight, commenting on "The True Story of Custer's Death" which was featured in a recent issue of the *Cosmopolitan Magazine.*[1]

There are about thirty men now living on the Tongue River Indian Reservation who actually took part in the bat-

---

[1]A similar statement was made by the Hunkpapa, Gall, during his visit to Custer Battlefield in 1886. See the *St. Paul Pioneer Press*, 7/18/1886.

tle. All of the Cheyenne warriors in the big camp on the Little Bighorn were in the attack on Custer as Custer's command was headed straight for the lower part of the camp occupied by the Cheyennes.

Willis Rowland in the government office here, has heard the story a great many times from the old men of the tribe as he has interpreted for writers, historians, and investigators of various kinds. According to the story told to Mr. Rowland by White Elk, now dead, Custer had his hair cut before the battle and could not have been recognized by his long hair.[2] Medicine Bear, who is also dead, claimed to have been the third Indian to "count coup" [on Gen. Custer] according to Indian custom.[3] He told at one time of seeing a Southern Cheyenne cut off General Custer's finger when he was unable to remove the ring.[4]

Mr. Rowland also pointed out that the Sioux Indians in Sitting Bull's band did not know General Custer as they had never seen him. The Cheyennes, on the other hand, had fought against him for several years in the southwest. A year or two before the fight on the Little Bighorn Custer held a council with the Cheyennes in the south at which he

---

[2]Born about 1849, White Elk was a combat veteran who participated in all the major Cheyenne engagements with the whites. He was a very brave man who had earned the right to wear a magnificent war bonnet. It was said that he was the owner of a powerful bird spirit, the swallow, which protected him during his valiant bravery runs in front of the enemy. He had an allotment near the confluence of Otter Creek and Tongue River and was still alive in 1915. See Marquis, *Wooden Leg,* 244; also Grinnell, *The Fighting Cheyennes,* 234.

In 1876, Gen. Custer was not only balding, but his hair was also cropped short before leaving on the expedition.

[3]Considered an act of great prowess among the Plains Indians, to count coup meant to touch the enemy during a combat situation, the act showing utter contempt for the opponent's martial abilities.

Little is known about Medicine Bear. Apparently, he was a respected individual who was allowed to carry the Turner, a sacred protector owned by the tribe, which had the power to turn bullets aside. In the 1890s, Medicine Bear was a member of the tribal Indian Police.

promised never to attack them. The peace pipe was pointed
to the four points of the compass and smoked by Custer and
the Cheyenne chiefs. The medicine man then laid a curse on
Custer, saying that if he ever fought against the Cheyennes
again he would be killed. The Cheyennes have always
believed that this was responsible for Custer's defeat.[5]

The Cheyennes never received any order from Sitting Bull
to spare General Custer. In the first place Sitting Bull did not
know Custer was in the country. The Indians had supposed
that the fighting had ended with the defeat of General Crook
at the bend of the Rosebud five [sic] days earlier. Sitting Bull
was not giving orders to the fighters. Two Moons, the leading chief of the Cheyennes, was in charge of the fighting
forces of the Cheyennes.

The story of the Indians silently awaiting the approach of
Custer and his command is absurd, according to Mr. Rowland. They did not know he was coming until they saw him.
Roan Bear, a Cheyenne, was the first to fire at Custer's command. Rising Fire also shot at them.[6] This firing aroused the
camp and directed the attention of the Indians to the soldiers

---

[4]Although containing some minor variations, a similar story was told by Kate Big Head,
the sister of the prominent Cheyenne, White Bull. Many years after the battle, she learned
from a Southern Cheyenne woman that only a finger joint was removed, and that the mutilation was done by a Lakota. However, those who identified Gen. Custer's remains failed to
mention this mutilation. Testimony revealed that Custer's body contained two bullet
wounds, one of which had crashed into the left temple, while the second projectile had
entered the rib cage, just below the heart. The mutilation of the corpse was only slight. The
left thigh had received a knife slash which had exposed the bone, while the genitals were
disfigured by an arrow. See Thomas B. Marquis, *Custer on the Little Bighorn* (Lodi, 1967),
43; and also Hardorff, *Custer Battle Casualties*, 30-31.

[5]This council took place near the forks of the Red River in present Oklahoma, in March
of 1869. See Jay Monaghan, *Custer: The Life of General George Armstrong Custer* (Lincoln,
1971), 329.

[6]Very little is known of either of these men. Roan Bear was a Kit Fox warrior and one of
the first to oppose Custer's command at Medicine Tail Ford. See Marquis, *Wooden Leg*,
230.

coming over the hill. The Cheyennes had been making preparations for going to the upper end of the camp where Reno and his men had been attacking the Sioux.

The Cheyennes believe firmly that Custer was the last to fall. They say that he was standing on higher ground than his men and could be seen above the smoke and dust. Before he was killed, however, he walked towards the place where the main body of his troops were making a stand. It would have been impossible to see whether he killed himself or was killed by the Indians.

According to the Indian version, Thunder Walking, a son of Chief White Bull, and Walking White Man rode into the midst of the troops while the fight was raging and fell headlong from their horses.[7]

A tradition of the Custer fight that is repeated by all the old warriors who took part is that the flag was taken from the soldier who was carrying it before he was killed, and [that it] was taken to the Cheyenne camp. Yellow Nose is said to have ridden through the soldiers in order to get the flag. The Indians were superstitious about the flag and did not allow it to touch the ground as they had observed the white soldiers treat it with respect.

Regarding the possibility of Sitting Bull knowing of Custer's approach, the Indians all say that they had no idea he was in the country. Their first knowledge that it was Custer

---

[7]The son of White Bull and Wool Woman, Thunder Walking, better known as Noisy Walking, was a young Cheyenne who was mortally wounded in Deep Ravine. He died during the night of June 25 in his parent's lodge.

Lame White Man was a respected Southern Cheyenne who was killed on the west slope of Custer Ridge, just below the rim, a short distance south of the present monument. Mistaking the body for that of an Arikara, the Minneconjou, Little Crow, removed the scalp lock—only to learn later that this individual was a Cheyenne, known to the Sioux by his Lakota name, Bearded Man. See Hardorff, *Hokahey! A Good Day to Die!*, 65-68, 76-78.

who had been killed was when he was recognized on the battlefield after his death by some of the Cheyennes who had met him in the south.

Little Wolf's band of Cheyennes were coming to join Sitting Bull's band from the Red Cloud Agency in Nebraska. The night before the battle they camped on the Rosebud near the present site of Busby [in Montana]. Two of his warriors, Black White Man and Big Crow went out to get game in the evening and saw a camp of soldiers.[8] They did not know who the soldiers were, but when they arose the next morning the soldiers had disappeared towards the west.

Little Wolf did not reach Sitting Bull's camp in time to warn him, so it is not probable that Sitting Bull or any of the chiefs in camp knew of the approach of the soldiers.

------

[8]According to George Bent, the name Black White Man was given to a Negro captive and which name was taken later by several noted Cheyennes. One was the signer of the Treaty of the Little Arkansas, in 1865, while a second individual by this name was a noted shaman in 1875. It was said that the uncle of George Bent also was known as Black White Man, he having taken this name as early as 1831. See Hyde, *Life of George Bent*, 64, 249; Marquis, *Wooden Leg*, 138; and Grinnell, *The Fighting Cheyennes*, 222.

Big Crow was a head soldier of the Crooked Lance Society and a man known for his bravery. In 1865, he led a decoy party near Old Julesburg which resulted in the killing of fourteen troopers. He displayed his bravery again during the capture of Dull Knife's village in 1876, but in January 1877, he was mortally wounded while defying the troops under Gen. Miles near the mouth of the Tongue River. See Hyde, *Life of George Bent*, 171; Grinnell, *The Fighting Cheyennes*, 183, 381; and Marquis, *Wooden Leg*, 290-91.

The Big Beaver Interview

INTRODUCTION

Big Beaver was a Northern Cheyenne who was born about 1859. Very little is known about him, which may be attributed in part to the fact that he was only a young boy at the time of the Custer Fight. Although his name is briefly mentioned in *Wooden Leg*, the history of this Cheyenne would have gone unnoticed if not for some brief moments in 1876, which are described in the interview which follows hereafter.

Born in Austria in 1883, Joseph A. Blummer and his parents immigrated to the United States of America the same year and settled in Springfield, Illinois. His father eventually homesteaded in Oelrichs, South Dakota; but after his mother's death in 1895, young Blummer took care of himself and settled on Pine Ridge with the Pete Shangrau family. Blummer worked as a cowboy for the Bar T Ranch until 1903, when a disastrous winter forced the cattle company into bankruptcy.

Blummer came to Montana in 1904, and for a while he was a stagecoach driver on the route between Crow Agency and Saint Xavier. Eventually, he became a rancher, and in the later years he operated the old Garryowen store which stood on the south side of the Garryowen Bend. Blummer's interest in the Custer Battle led to his discovery of Custer's trail from Luce Ridge to Calhoun Hill. Although this location is named Nye-Cartwright Ridge, it was

BIG BEAVER STANDS NEAR MARKER #174 FARTHEST EAST ON THE BATTLEFIELD
This marks the site where he witnessed the killing of a lone soldier
who failed in his attempted escape from Custer Ridge.
Photograph was taken by Dr. Thomas B. Marquis in August 1927.
Photo courtesy of Custer Battlefield National Monument, National Park Service.

Blummer who made the initial discovery of casings at this site and who notified the authorities of his find. However, Blummer never received any credit for this historically important discovery.

The following is a transcript of the interview held with Big Beaver in 1928. It is contained in the Joseph A. Blummer Manuscript, Item A-123, housed at Custer Battlefield National Monument, which acquired the manuscript in 1957. Although the Blummer Manuscript consists of more than 100 pages of typescript, the text of the interview is contained on pages 52-54. In the following transcript, I have corrected errors in spelling and grammar which appeared in the original, and have provided paragraphing and punctuation which were lacking.

THE BIG BEAVER INTERVIEW
Custer Battlefield, Montana, 1928

Dr. Thomas Marquis and I had done much investigation of the Custer and Reno battles. Dr. Marquis was the doctor at Lame Deer for several years, and he became one of the best sign language talkers that I ever came in contact with. While at Lame Deer, he became acquainted with quite a few Cheyenne Indians who were in the Custer and Reno battles. And having befriended some of them, he gained their confidence and gradually, a little at a time, they would tell about the Custer battle. For a long [time], the old Indians were afraid that the government would punish them if the government found out which ones were in the battle. Now, the Doctor and I were quite intimate friends, and he told me lots of things in confidence. It took him two years before he could find out much about the fights.[1]

I will now take up the story of Big Beaver as told to us in the summer of 1928. Dr. Thomas Marquis and Big Beaver came to my place, the store at Garryowen, Montana, and were there with me three days, and each day we would go over the battlefields and Big Beaver would tell us what he knew about the battle and what he saw. He was very careful to tell us each time as to what he saw, or whether it was something he heard the other Indians say. I will only give the part he says he saw or took part in.

The first he remembers is that [which took place] on the day the soldiers came. In those days, the Indians had no way of telling the days or months or time of day as we use them. We have to take it [therefore] the way they remember it, or their way of expressing it. Word was brought that soldiers were coming to fight them. He says he was about seventeen years old at the time. He started to get his pony to go in the fight. His father told him, "Son, you are too young to fight, and as there are lots of fighting men there, they will not need you." But he went anyway, having only a bow and arrows, as up to this time he never had a gun. He says many Indians in the fight did not have a gun.[2]

As the Cheyenne camp was the one on the north or lower end of the great Indian camp, this made them the nearest to the [Custer] battleground. He says all the Indians from this end of the camp went north along the river, thence to the right or east, and came up towards Custer from the north side. When he got there, he left his pony back some distance and crawled up the coulee just north and a little to the east of where the present monument is. He described a Sioux with a

---

[1]Born in Missouri in 1869, Dr. Thomas B. Marquis was the agency physician for the Northern Cheyennes at Lame Deer, Montana, from 1922 until 1931. His interest in and his intimate knowledge of the Cheyennes and their way of life resulted in a number of historical publications, chief among which was Wooden Leg's biography. Dr. Marquis passed away in 1935, after suffering from a heart ailment. His remains are buried at Custer Battlefield National Cemetery, Grave site C-2.

[2]For a discussion of the different types of Indian firearms , see Douglas D . Scott and Richard A. Fox, Jr. , *Archaeological Insights into the Custer Battle* (Norman, 1987), 108-13; and also Douglas D. Scott, et al., *Archaeological Perspectives on the Battle of the Little Bighorn* (Norman, 1989) , 153-66, 175-83.

warbonnet as being just ahead of him. This Sioux would jump up and shoot towards the soldiers on the hill where the monument is; then he would fall down and reload, and crawl ahead again. He did this several times. Big Beaver said he was close behind him when he jumped up to shoot again when a bullet struck him in the forehead. He then described just where the bullet hit the Sioux. Then he said, "I thought it was no place for me," so he turned and crawled back.[3]

Then he says a soldier got up and mounted his horse (this was one of [Capt. Myles] Keogh's men, or Sorrel Horse Troop), and rode as fast as he could towards the east.[4] This is the lone marker next to the fence to the east of the Keogh position. Two Cheyenne Indians cut him off and killed him. He then described how they scalped him and hung the scalp on the sagebrush. He says he then went over there and got the gun and some other things, and that was the first gun he ever owned.[5]

When he returned to where the other Indians were in the coulee, he saw them all rushing up towards the hill where the

---

[3]This incident is described in *Wooden Leg*, 236, but the text, however, identifies Wooden Leg as the eyewitness.

[4]Sorrel horses were assigned to Troop C; Keogh's I Troop rode bay horses .

[5]The location of this kill site is known to battlefield personnel as Marker 174, which site yielded the following artifacts during the 1984 survey: three spent 45/55 casings, one Colt revolver cartridge, one Colt bullet which was vertically impacted into the ground, and one deformed 50/70 slug. Archaeologists speculate that this individual was able to defend himself for a short while with his carbine. However, subsequent pressure by the arriving Indians did not allow him time to reload, upon which he resorted to his revolver. He was apparently shot while drawing his Colt because his convulsive reaction discharged the revolver into the ground. See Scott and Fox, Jr., *Archaeological Insights*, 124.

In *Wooden Leg*, Marquis describes this very same incident, but he names as his informant not Big Beaver, but rather Wooden Leg, and, for unexplained reasons, Marquis changes the homicide to a suicide! In light of these irregularities, one wonders about the credibility of the suicide theory of which Marquis was an avid believer. See Marquis, *Wooden Leg*, 233-34. The suicide theory is developed in Marquis, *Keep the Last Bullet for Yourself* (New York, 1976).

monument is. He stated that he went up also, and when he got up there no soldiers were standing up, but some were still firing that were on the ground or sitting up. The Indians rushed them, and that was the end there, but, he says, some men, about fifteen, got up over to the west, or on the E Troop position, and ran for the river, right down the coulee. He says these soldiers were scared as they did not shoot back, and that the Indians ran them down.[6] Now, these men were out of ammunition and could not shoot back [and] they were trying to make it to the brush along the river. That is the way he saw it, he says—they just ran towards the river. To me, these men made a rush towards the river to try to save themselves by hiding in the brush on the riverbank. My idea is that they used all their ammunition and were making this last effort to get away. These markers [for these slain men] are the last seventeen markers down the coulee , southeast [southwest] of the monument. [7]

He knew nothing about the rest of the battlefield as , he says , the smoke and the dust were so thick he could not see very far. All the Indians from farther back had come upon the field by this time and everyone was trying to get something . On June 26 , he was up at the Reno field but did nothing there as he could not get near the troops.

---

[6]Blummer's comment about the E Troop position has reference to a location near Deep Ravine where allegedly the whole of E Troop was found after the battle. Blummer undoubtedly obtained his information from Thomas Marquis who concluded that it was here that E Troop committed suicide en masse, although he later wrote that this incident took place at the *beginning* of the battle, and that the identity of the annihilated troop was uncertain. Despite Blummer's assertion that the soldiers seen by Big Beaver fled from Deep Ravine, it seems more likely that these men came from Custer Hill, from which Big Beaver made his observation moments after the troopers had fled. See the statement by the Oglala, He Dog, in Hammer, *Custer in '76*, 207, and also the observations by the Minneconjou, Standing Bear, and the Hunkpapa, Iron Hawk, in DeMallie, *The Sixth Grandfather*, 186, 191. See also Marquis, *Wooden Leg*, 231-32.

[7]It is interesting to note that Two Moons made a similar statement about these markers during his interview with J.M. Thrall in 1901.

The Young Two Moons Interview

INTRODUCTION

Born in 1855, Young Two Moons was the son of Beaver Claws and a maternal grandson of Elk River who was one of the most respected men among the Northern Cheyennes. Beaver Claws was the older half brother of Chief Two Moons after whom Young Two Moons was named. After his father's death in 1905, Young Two Moons took care of his ailing uncle whom he accompanied on his last visit to Custer Battlefield in 1916. Chief Two Moons passed away in 1917, while his nephew, also known as John Two Moons, was still alive as late as 1937.

The name of Stanley Vestal needs very little introduction. Born as Walter S. Campbell in rural Kansas in 1887, his family eventually moved to Guthrie, Oklahoma Territory, where he developed a lasting interest in the Plains Indian. Campbell was a Rhodes Scholar and accepted a faculty position with the University of Oklahoma in 1915, which institution he served for more than forty years. He also served with the armed forces in southern France during World War I in 1918 and 1919. He was a novelist, a biographer, a historian, a master teacher of writers, and above all, an exhaustive researcher. Campbell published twenty-four books, some 150 journal and magazine articles, and five radio scripts. He is perhaps best known for his work, *Sitting Bull, Champion of the*

Sioux. Campbell passed away in 1957, and was buried at Custer Battlefield National Cemetery, Grave Site C-658.

The following is a transcript of the original manuscript contained in the Walter Stanley Campbell Collection, Box 105, Notebook 15, University of Oklahoma Libraries, pages 1-42, which carries the heading, "C[uster] Bat[tlefield] Trip." The text is recorded in longhand and contains numerous abbreviations. For the benefit of the reader, I have changed the abbreviations into completed words and have corrected errors in spelling and grammar. I have also provided paragraphing and punctuation which was lacking in the original. It should be noted further that the original manuscript was not dated. However, I was able to determine the year of origin from the information provided in Campbell's biographical notes.

THE YOUNG TWO MOONS INTERVIEW
Custer Battlefield, Montana, 1929

Plenty Bears, a Sioux, was buried in teepee [on Reno Creek]. He was shot in the guts and died that night and was buried on flat, and parents returned same day [to Little Bighorn]. Parents later returned and found big shod horse tracks all around it.[1]

One of Little Wolf's men, Black White Man, saw split in Custer's command.[2]

Many women were digging tipsin across the Little Bighorn that morning. No soldiers were expected. On June 24, Box Elder, a Cheyenne prophet [also known as] Dog Stands on Ridge, sent a crier to warn the people to hold their horses [in readiness]. He saw soldiers coming; but people did not listen because they did not believe it.[3]

During travel, [Old] Two Moons led, and Sitting Bull was in charge of the rear. Indians held Reno['s force] for two

[1]The name Plenty Bears may well have been the Cheyenne name of this Lakota. However, there exists some confusion about the identity of this slain man. The wife of the Hunkpapa, Kills Assiniboine, recalled that the victim's name was Sitting Bear, while the Minneconjou, Feather Earring, stated that the body was that of Old She Bear. Feather Earring added further that the victim—a brother of the Sans Arc, Circling Bear, or Turning Bear—had died from a gunshot through both hips and was left on a scaffold in a lodge on Reno Creek. The Oglala, He Dog, affirmed that the slain man was Turning Bear's brother, a Sans Arc, and that he had died from a gunshot to the bowels, but he did not reveal the man's name. To add to the confusion, Army officers were told by enlisted Oglalas in 1878, that a skull found on Reno Creek was that of the Hunkpapa, Little Wing, a casualty of the Rosebud Fight. In view of the diversity in names, it is possible that more than one Lakota burial took place on Reno Creek, which was suggested by the Cheyenne, American Horse. This appears to be supported also by Lt. Charles A. Varnum who claimed to have seen two lodges on Reno Creek from the observation post on the divide. However, since this sighting was made at daybreak, it may well be that the second lodge was occupied by the grieving parents of the deceased, as indicated by Young Two Moons. It should be noted further that all other contemporary sources confirm the existence of a single lodge, containing only one body. This is indirectly supported by the Lakotas, who knew immediately that the skull found among the camp debris was that of Little Wing. Unfortunately, the names of neither Sitting Bear, Old She Bear, nor Little Wing appear on a list prepared by White Bull. According to the latter, a literate Minneconjou Lakota, the names of the slain Sioux were: Black Bird, Little Crow, Little Wolf, and Standing Bear. Although the Cheyenne, Wooden Leg, confided to Marquis that as many as 20 Lakotas were killed in the Rosebud Fight, White Bull's dead count of only four is independently corroborated by the Hunkpapa, Old Bull, and also by William Garnett who had Oglala family ties. It is perhaps possible that some of the aforesaid names were nicknames for some of the casualties on White Bull's list. I should further mention that I was unable to reconcile any of the Lakota names mentioned by Feather Earring, which makes me wonder whether the latter deliberately changed the names to protect the true identity for reasons only known to him. Regardless of what the nickname may have been, the most revealing information on this subject came from the Hunkpapa, Has Horns. He told Walter Camp in 1912 that the slain Lakota left on Reno Creek was Little Wolf, a Sans Arc, whose name is indeed listed on the White Bull roster. Has Horns added further that the watercourse now known as Reno Creek was named Little Wolf Creek by the Sans Arc, which geographical identification honors the memory of this slain tribesman. See Graham, *The Custer Myth*, 98; Hammer, *Custer in '76*, 205; Camp Manuscripts, Indiana University, 357; Marquis, *Wooden Leg*, 202-03; Robert A. Clark, *The Killing of Chief Crazy Horse* (Lincoln 1989), 110; and John M. Carroll, *A Seventh Cavalry Scrapbook, #10* (Bryan, 1979), 13

[2]It is unsure whether the observation refers to the dispatch of Benteen's battalion at the divide at noon, or whether it refers to the dispatch of Reno's battalion at the Lone Tepee some two hours later.

[3]Born about 1790, Box Elder was a famous prophet among the Northern Cheyennes who predicted the future. It was said that both he and his son, Brave Wolf, gained this knowledge through the wolves and that both men possessed this power in a high degree. Ironically, in November of 1876, a blind Box Elder predicted the destruction of Dull Knife's

nights. Indians did not shoot horses.[4] Orders were to mourn and not to dance on Little Bighorn, and go up Little Bighorn afterwards. Two miles downstream soldiers came up and entrenched, so there was no fight.[5] We then moved tribes from Little Bighorn. Indians stayed together after this. We caught [some] whites in mountains on Tongue River. But they escaped in the night and left their horses.[6]

After the Custer battle, the women moved from the bend and pitched their lodges helter skelter, some on the hills to the west.

How many Indians had guns in the Custer Fight?

We were pretty well armed. A real good horse bought a gun. One mule brought a gun. Hard to get guns—gun sellers wanted mules. Traders travelling through with pack mules and [traded] robes for muzzle loaders and later rimfire Winchesters. Indians had many 45 and 50 caliber guns and Winchesters at time of Custer Fight.

Ever traded across the Missouri at the forts?

No. Two Moons belonged to a wild bunch and did not

village, but as a result of the interference by the Kit Fox Society, the prophecy was ignored with disastrous results. Box Elder, also known as Old Brave Wolf and Horn, died about 1885. See Grinnell, *The Cheyenne Indians*, II, 107, 112.

There exists some confusion about the name Brave Wolf which was probably caused by Grinnell who wrote that "Brave Wolf was also known as Maple, or Box Elder." Of course, the Brave Wolf spoken of was actually Old Brave Wolf, then known as Horn, he having passed his name on to his son. See Stands in Timber and Liberty, *Cheyenne Memories*, 215, 216.

[4]The siege of Reno Hill resulted in the killing of some forty-six horses and mules, some of which attributable to mercy killings by Army personnel. See the *Bismarck Tribune*, 11/2/1877.

[5]Reference is made to the Montana Column which camped near present Crow Agency, on June 26, some two miles below Custer's battlefield. See Edward J. McClernand, *With the Indian and the Buffalo*, 59.

[6]This was the Sibley Fight which took place near the headwaters of the Little Bighorn, July 7, 1876. The exact location may have been near the head of Nickel Creek where many years later pieces of harness leather and rusted metal were discovered. See Hila Gilbert, "*Big Bat" Pourier* (Sheridan, 1968), 81.

reach posts. Traded with traders, sometimes before fighting with whites. Oklahoma Indians fought down south and then came north and got us into trouble.[7] Whites jumped on bands whether the right one or not.

Two moons was twenty-one in 1876. Were you with your uncle [Old Two Moons] all the time?

No.

The Gray Horse Company moved from the south onto top of the ridge. Walking White [Man's] party made first charge, on side of hill. Yellow Nose was close by. Both drive soldiers [onto?] top. Two Moons came northeast over the hill, yelling, and soldiers ran west down ridge toward the river. [See map.]

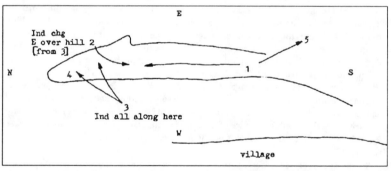

LAYOUT OF CUSTER RIDGE, POSSIBLY DRAWN BY TWO MOONS

Two Moons at "2". Walking White [Man's] party and Yellow Nose at "1".[8] Rest of Indians at "3".

---

[7] The Oklahoma Indians were the Southern Cheyennes who raided the Platte Valley before moving into the Powder River region after the Sand Creek Massacre in 1864. As a result of the Indian raids, the Army organized an expedition which was to operate north of the Platte to hunt the Indians "like wolves." This force consisted of three columns, led by Col. Nelson Cole, Col. Samuel Walker, and Gen. Patrick E. Conner, and although the Army surprised an Arapahoe camp, in the end the expedition accomplished nothing. It did, however, solidify the Indian resistance to white encroachment which resulted in a decisive Indian victory near Fort Kearny, late in 1866. For a detailed Indian view of these turbulent years, see Hyde, *Life of George Bent*, 164-243.

.All met at "4" on west side of the hill. Sixty gravestones at this location, Custer slightly above, all in one bunch, covering about one acre, and some scattered down the valley.

They had dirt on their stomachs, but were not buried for three years.[9]

[Lt. Henry M.] Harrington [escaped] one mile toward "5".[10] I don't know where Gall was.

The Cheyennes came from the east and chased [the soldiers] southwest, and then closed in on the remainder.

Custer waved saber and [then] soldiers shot.

Custer's finger cut off to get ring off by 3 to cc [?].

Indians on all sides.

---

[8]Variously identified as Walking White and Crippled White Man, Lame White Man was the head soldier of the Elk Society and a man of much influence among the Northern Cheyennes. At the Little Bighorn, he took a leading part in the assault on Calhoun Hill, driving the surviving troopers in confusion toward Custer Hill. Some distance southwest of the present monument, he furiously charged amidst the troopers on the ridge and was mortally wounded by a gunshot through the breast. Mistaking the body for that of an Arikara Indian, the Hunkpapa, Little Crow, removed Lame White Man's scalp, while others inflicted numerous stab wounds on the remains. Lame White Man was known among the Lakotas as Bearded Man, or Moustache. Although some accounts state that he was an "Old Man" tribal chief, his age (37) and his active position of war chief would have prevented him from serving in the prestigious office of tribal leader simultaneously. See Marquis, *Wooden Leg*, 211, 242; Walter Camp Manuscripts, 366-67; *Billings Gazette*, 5/26/1927; and Vestal, *Warpath*, 199.

[9]In the spring of 1879, Capt. George K. Sanderson and a company were dispatched from Fort Custer to reinter all exposed remains on Custer Battlefield. In addition, they collected all horse bones in a hollow square formed by a cordwood monument erected on Custer Hill. Two years later, this wooden structure was replaced by a commemorative obelisk. See Hardorff, *Custer Battle Casualties*, 67.

[10]Lt. Harrington commanded C Troop, its senior officer, Capt. Thomas W. Custer, having been assigned to serve on headquarters staff as an aid-de-camp to his brother. Because Harrington was declared MIA, his fate has been the subject of continued speculation, including the suggestion he had deserted the field of combat. Such charges are unfounded and unjustly malign the character of an officer who had an excellent military record. Most likely, Harrington's body was not identified due to extreme mutilation, and probably decapitation. It should be noted that Thomas Custer would probably also have been declared MIA if not for the initials "TWC" tattooed on his arm. See Hardorff, *Custer Battle Casualties*, 98-99.

The Indians say if Custer had gone northwest he had better show.

One man went south (almost southwest) and almost got away. A Cheyenne, Bear Tail, and a Sioux got him.[11]

Red Robe and [Sgt. James] Butler fought hand-to-hand east of south end.[12]

There was lots of unfired ammunition on the soldiers.

June 25, 1876, was a hot, clear day and no wind. There was a great dust from fighting, but no storm after the battle.

To the north of Custer's position is a far-off ridge [which runs] to the dark green line of timber below. Barren hills to the east, covered with sagebrush. To the west [are] steep slopes and lapping ridges, with timber tops beyond bluffs and flats and flat-topped hills, and far away the blue, snow-spotted peaks of the Big Horn Mountains. To the south are masses of timber on the flats, and beyond the green-yellow ridges and the brown hill (Reno Hill), and far away the rugged Wolf Mountains, crested with stately pines.[13]

Did the Cheyennes have 200 warriors?

I don't know.

---

[11]The Cheyenne, Bear Tail, may have been the same individual identified by White Shield as Old Bear. Stands in Timber in *Cheyenne Memories*, 207-08, tells of a similar incident in which the Oglala, Low Dog, and the Cheyenne, Little Sun, were involved.

[12]This Cheyenne has not been positively identified. It was said that an individual by this name had lost his only two sons during a battle with the Crow Indians, and that he had attempted to "throw his life away" on several occasions. Eventually, the deaths of his two sons were avenged by Two Twists, head soldier of the Bow String Society, who consequently was adopted by Red Robe as his son. See K.N. Llewellyn and E.A. Hoebel, *The Cheyenne Way: Conflict and Case Law in Primitive Jurisprudence* (Norman, 1941), 3, 6.

Born in Albany, New York, in 1842, James Butler was a first sergeant in L Troop and had served in the Seventh Cavalry since 1870. Of courageous character, Butler was found on the heights southwest of Luce Ridge, his mutilated corpse lying amidst numerous cartridge shells. See Hammer, *Men With Custer*, 228.

[13]This description was given, of course, by Walter Campbell who made his observation from Custer Hill, although from this location Reno Hill is not visible.

How many Cheyenne lodges?

Two hundred lodges, and three warriors to a lodge. There were six Arapahoes with the Cheyennes, but they did not have teepees.[14]

What was the length of the moving camp?

I don't know. Leaders have teepee set up miles in advance before the last ones have teepees in camp. Leaders are on horse, always ready for attack, and band warriors go around singing to keep spirits up. Hard to find a lost horse. Get on hill and watch camp go by. Moving camp is half a mile wide. Scouts are out all the time. Camps take turn.

Scouts said that Custer tried to encircle camp, but that he did not have enough men. On Custer day there were no scouts, but horse guards. There were many horses north of the river on the hills. The Two Moon family had forty head.

To carry teepee and eighteen poles takes one horse. Eighteen buffalo skins is eighteen poles.

Middle aged and young in fight. Many Indians not in fight; so remainder charge Reno while Custer battle is on. Reno crossed between two bunches of bands. Mules ran for water, scared, but Indians got some with packs on.[15] There

---

[14] The number of Arapahoes present at the Little Bighorn amounted to a war party of only six young men who had left Fort Robinson on a foray against the Shoshones. While en route, they were discovered and detained by Lakotas who suspected them to be scouts for the U.S. Army. However, through the intervention of the Cheyennes—particularly Two Moons who had Arapahoe relatives—these six captives were released and they subsequently took part in the Custer Battle. The accounts of two of these men may be found in Graham, *The Custer Myth*, 109-12.

[15] As a result of the confusion on Reno Hill, a number of mules were allowed to wander off to the river and were caught by the Indians. Among these mules were two loaded with ammunition boxes, and although Sgt. Richard P. Hanley earned a Medal of Honor by catching one of these animals, the other one, with its precious cargo, fell into the hands of the Lakotas. See Frank Linderman, *Pretty-Shield* (Lincoln, 1972), 240; Melbourne C. Chandler, *Of Garry Owen in Glory: The History of the Seventh United States Cavalry Regiment* (Annandale, 1960), 397; Marquis, *Wooden Leg*, 262-63.

were no dead soldiers east of river on flat.[16] But there was some hand-to-hand [fighting] and some soldiers got [killed] in river.[17] After two nights quit [fighting]. Ridges sprawling to river.

Women left teepees standing when they ran [upon Reno's attack]. After Reno retreated, some returned to get their things, but ran again when Custer Fight started. Teepees were made out of buffalo hides. Red Cloud and Blue Horse had canvas teepees instead.[18]

Why did he [Red Cloud] not come here?

No! Wouldn't let them [the agency Indians] come against the white men nor join Sitting Bull.

U.S. Government punished some Sawtaw [Santees] by cutting rim off ear. Sitting Bull was mad. Don't know his name, but did see ears, yes. [Santees] camped in own bunch next to Sitting Bull's camp.[19]

---

[16]Reference is probably made to the flat east of Reno's retreat crossing, which did contain the remains of several troopers, among which was Lt. Benjamin Hodgson who was Reno's adjutant. See Hardorff, *Custer Battle Casualties*, 127-30.

[17]One of those who was involved in hand-to-hand combat was the Minneconjou, One Bull, who, armed with a club, killed two troopers in the river and a third one on the east bank at the retreat crossing. See the One Bull Interview, Walter Campbell Collection, Box 105, Notebook 19.

[18]Born east of the Black Hills in 1821, Red Cloud was the dominant leader of the Bad Face Band of the Oglalas. He is perhaps best known for his determined resistance against the establishment of forts on the Bozeman Trail along the eastern slope of the Big Horn Mountains. Rightfully named Red Cloud's War, the hostilities led to the abandonment of these military posts in 1868. After signing the Fort Laramie Treaty in the same year, Red Cloud resigned himself to reservation life and remained at peace with the whites until his death on December 10, 1909. For biographical data on this great Lakota, see George Hyde, *Red Cloud's Folk* (Norman, 1937), and also James C. Olson, *Red Cloud and the Sioux Problem* (Lincoln, 1965). Blue Horse was an Oglala band leader and a close ally of Red Cloud.

[19]After the Sioux uprising in Minnesota in 1862, many of the Santees moved west across the Missouri and eventually found sanctuary in Canada. In the fall of 1875, some 20 Santee lodges under Old Red Top crossed the border and joined the Hunkpapas and subsequently participated in the Custer Battle. I have been unable to find any corroborating evidence on the alleged charge of mutilation.

Was Sitting Bull hard hearted?

In fight, yes. He hated to see idle warriors. The only thing which smelled good to Sitting Bull was gunpowder. Sitting Bull was good-hearted, but he loved to kill. Whites could not kill him, but [it took a] Sioux to get rid of him.[20] The Cheyenne, Little Wolf, same as Sitting Bull—kills his victim, then laughs as his victim dies. Older people have seen Sitting Bull kill people. Sitting Bull urged with effect and could bluff warriors into battle. No bluff—Indians go where he commanded others.

In spring of 1876, Cheyennes were in Powder River Fight where they lost horses. From Powder River they then went to mouth of Otter Creek, and from Otter Creek to Pumpkin Creek, and there in the brakes found a Sioux camp, but got nothing.

In Blue Mountains, on Beaver Creek (near Powder River), they found Sitting Bull's camp. He gave the Cheyennes horses and some teepees. From Beaver Creek they went to Tongue River where Sitting Bull summoned all the tribes to [join] on Rosebud Creek. On the Rosebud, Sitting Bull sent [runners] out for horses. He said, "Don't spare anyone; if you meet anyone, kill him and take his horses. Save nothing."

On Rosebud Creek, Two Moons and Sitting Bull were chosen as leaders of the camp. Sitting Bull never wanted to give up or surrender. [After the Custer Fight] Sitting Bull went across the Yellowstone and he did not see the

---

[20]Sitting Bull was killed while resisting arrest near the present town of Bullhead, South Dakota, December 15, 1890. According to Walter Campbell, Sitting Bull was instantly killed by a gunshot fired by Bull Head, a member of the Standing Rock Indian Police. However, the Hunkpapa Gray Eagle, a witness to the shooting, told Walter Camp that Bull Head did not fire at Sitting Bull, but that the latter was killed by Sgt. Red Tomahawk who had fired his pistol at Sitting Bull's heart. See Vestal, *Sitting Bull*, 300; and Walter Camp Manuscripts, 343.

Cheyennes after that. Hunkpapas and Cheyennes were always friendly [to each other].

[Old] Red Cloud not in Custer Fight. Blue Horse nothing like Sitting Bull—wanted Red Cloud to keep Indians quiet and not to join Sitting Bull.

Two Moons knows Crazy Horse.

Was Crazy Horse bulletproof?

I don't know.

Was Crazy Horse great?

He was brave. He and Low Dog and (Buffalo) Hump were three brave Sioux fighters.

The Medicine Arrows and [Sacred] Hat were in the Custer Fight. The Sioux on Pumpkin Creek went with them to Sitting Bull's camp.

Two Moons did not get any guns or horses in the Custer Fight. Men in the rear [went] after horses. An enemy horse is your property when you touch or hold it.

Was there a Sioux woman fighter in the Custer Battle?

I don't know.[21]

Was there a Cheyenne woman fighter?

Yes. During Crook Fight [on Rosebud] a girl followed her brother, Chief Comes in Sight. Her name was Calf Road. Her brother's horse was killed and he was saved [by riding] double with his sister. This girl was a good rider. They were both from Oklahoma.[22]

---

[21]This was Moving Robe Woman who fought Custer's troopers to avenge the death of a relative. When the battle was over, she had killed two of Custer's men— shooting one soldier and hacking the second one to death with a sheath knife. Moving Robe Woman was born in 1854, and was the daughter of the Hunkpapa, Crawler. Her account of the Custer Battle may be found in Hardorff, *Lakota Recollections*, 91-96

[22]Buffalo Calf Trail Woman was the sister of Chief Comes in Sight whose life she saved at the Rosebud Fight. Hence, the Cheyennes call this the Battle Where the Girl Saved Her

Little Bighorn a good place for mosquitoes. Few that year.
Ash-gray bluffs and thin timber to the northeast beyond the
Little Bighorn. Flats to the north, and a slew to the south and
not so much water. Green-brown hills to the north and one
snow peak of the Big Horn Mountains is seen to the south of
southwest.[23]

Terrible plague of flies that summer. Bodies of slain Indians blown with maggots during the short time that the fight
lasted.

(Old men ushers on trail as [they] come into a camp. All
mixed up on trail.) Young men (people) travel on edge of
moving camp.

Burials.

Crow [Indians] dig hole in which they sit deceased, head
sticking out, the body dressed in clothes.[24]

Sioux and Cheyennes [are buried] on four poles. [Body
of] Cheyenne [is placed] on right side, with knees bent, as in

Brother. She also fought in the Custer Battle and it was said that she again distinguished
herself by shooting several troopers. As a result of these gallant deeds she was given the
name of Brave Woman. Nonetheless, her personal life was full of tragedy. She had married
Black Coyote, a man who came from a distinguished fighting family, but who was always
full of anger and who had very little self control. After murdering a Cheyenne chief in 1878,
Black Coyote went immediately into exile, being followed by Buffalo Calf Trail Woman
and their two children, one a newborn infant. In the same year, Black Coyote was captured
by soldiers and imprisoned at Fort Keogh for depredations against whites. While in Oklahoma Territory in 1877, Buffalo Trail Calf Woman had been stricken by a Malarial disease,
and as a result of the hardships imposed onto her by her husband's exile, her weakened condition was unable to resists the effects of the disease. She died near Fort Keogh, Montana
Territory, in 1878. Thus passed away a Cheyenne woman whose devotion and loyalty to her
family deserves the admiration of all.

For biographical data on Chief Comes in Sight and Buffalo Calf Trail Woman, see
Grinnell, *The Cheyenne Indians*, I, 157, II, 44; Marquis, *Cheyennes and Sioux*, 16; Llewellyn
and Hoebel, *The Cheyenne Way*, 174-75. Marquis, *Wooden Leg*, 211, 301, 329-30; and Grinnell, *The Fighting Cheyennes*, 336.

[23]This description was given by Walter Campbell at the location of the Hunkpapa camp
circle, just north of the Garryowen Bend.

sleep. The dead [Cheyenne] Indians were buried west across river and the flat.

What do you know about the lodge and drum story?

Don't know, but Sioux drummer [was] with drum.[25]

[What was the reputation] of Pawnee fighters?

Good.

Ute fighters?

Better.

Arapahoe fighters?

Pretty good scrappers.

Did Cheyennes fight Flatheads?

Yes. Cheyennes fought with all but the Blackfeet. Cheyennes and Arapahoes lived together for many years. Northern Arapahoes [are called] Sage Men. Southern Ara-

---

[24]One such Crow Indian burial had taken place on the west bank near Reno's retreat crossing. The burial pit was in the hollow created by the root system of a dead cottonwood tree, and it was said to have contained the body of a clothed female, in sitting position, and an infant. About 1906, these remains were exhumed and reintered at the Custer Battlefield National Cemetery. See the Joe A. Blummer Manuscript, 33-34, Custer Battlefield National Monument.

[25]The "lodge and drum story" probably has reference to a drum found in the middle of the deserted Lakota camps along the Little Bighorn. On the west side of this drum several dead Lakotas were found lying on a blanket. This discovery was made by the Arikara, Young Hawk, who added that a tepee had stood over the bodies and the drum, but that soldiers destroyed the lodge and slashed the drum. See O.G. Libby, *The Arikara Narrative of the Campaign against the Hostile Dakotas, June, 1876* (New York, 1973), 109.

The John Stands in Timber Interview

INTRODUCTION

Born in 1884, John Stands in Timber was the oldest son of Stands Different and Buffalo Cow Woman, and a maternal grandson of Lame White Man, a Cheyenne war chief who was slain during the Custer Fight. Stands in Timber was educated at the reservation mission school and later attended the Haskell Institute at Lawrence, Kansas. During his lifetime he was engaged in various trades. He was an engineering assistant in government schools; a cowboy who herded tribal cattle herds; an independent farmer; a leader in reservation politics; and above all, he was a Mennonite Christian who helped build the Mission at Birney in 1908.

His main interest in life was the tribal history of his people, and for that reason he elected himself tribal historian. Throughout his life he collected information from the Cheyenne elders with the hope to someday publish this information. With the assistance of Margot Liberty, an anthropologist, Stands in Timber's dream became a reality. In 1966, Yale University Press accepted *Cheyenne Memories* for publication, but as the book went to press in 1967, John Stands in Timber passed away.

Don Rickey, Jr., was the Chief Historian at Custer Battlefield

National Monument in the 1950s and early 1960s. He is an expert on firearms used during the Indian Wars period, and is the author of the classic work, *Forty Miles a Day on Beans and Hay: The Enlisted Soldiers Fighting the Indian Wars*, published in 1963. The following transcript is a copy of an interview held by Don Rickey, Jr., with Stands in Timber, which is housed at the Custer Battlefield National Monument, and it is hereby reproduced with their permission. The editing consists mainly of paragraphing.

THE JOHN STANDS IN TIMBER INTERVIEW
Custer Battlefield, Montana, 1956

This informant, now seventy years old, spent much time gathering data on the Battle of the Little Bighorn from Cheyenne participants, including his grandfather, Wolf Tooth. His other grandfather, Lame White Man, was killed in the battle. Stands in Timber is educated, and he made written notes on his information after returning from school as a young man fifty years ago. Through the offices of Mr. J. W. Vaughn, an attorney of Winsor, Colorado, Stands in Timber was brought to the battlefield where he related his information to Mr. Vaughn and Historian [Don] W. Rickey.[1]

Lame White Man's widow, Stands in Timber's grandmother, was named Twin Woman, and her brother was Tall Bull (Cheyenne) who was also in the battle and provided some of the information. Wolf Tooth (informant's other grandfather) took Stands in Timber over the battlefield about forty years ago and showed him where Lame White Man and Noisy Walking were found dead after the fight. These places have been marked with stakes.[2]

---

[1]Through his avocational pursuit, Jesse W. Vaughn pioneered the use of metal detecting devices on many western Indian War battlefields. Before his death in 1968, he had authored four scholarly works based on his field findings, among which was *With Crook on the Rosebud* (Harrisburg: 1956) which is probably his best known.

The chiefs in the fight were all equal. The leading warrior was Crazy Horse—also Gall, Iron Thunder, Two Moons, American Horse (Cheyenne), Dull Knife, Little Wolf, Crazy Head and Red Cloud (a Cheyenne-Sioux, not related to the Ogalala chief).[3]

The village first knew of Custer's approach when Long Dog and Red Tomahawk saw the troops at their second camp on the route up the Rosebud. The village was then at the site of Busby. The Indians watched the soldiers constantly from then on.[4] The day before the battle (June 24), village criers announced that no man was to leave camp, and that

---

[2]About 1916, the kill site of Lame White Man was marked by a small pile of stones in accordance with a time-honored custom. As a result of Stands in Timber's information, the National Park Service placed an interpretive sign at this spot in 1956, the marker simply stating that Lame White Man had been slain near this location. This kill site is along Custer Ridge, on the river side of the present blacktop, a short distance south of Custer Hill.

The kill site of the young Cheyenne, Noisy Walking, was also marked in 1916. In 1990, I was shown this location by battlefield personnel. The site was marked by some flat rocks, well buried now in the sandy soil. The location is due west of the Lame White Marker, about halfway between Custer Ridge and the head of Deep Ravine. However, I have considerable doubt about this location because all contemporary sources, including Noisy Walking's aunt, Howling Woman, state that the young man was found on the bottom of Deep Ravine, near the river. See Hardorff, *Hokahey! A Good Day to Die!*, 68-69, 77.

[3]Crazy head was a noted warrior and later became one of the important tribal leaders of the Northern Cheyennes. He had been a war chief who led a Cheyenne band in the Fetterman Fight of 1866. He was present at the Little Bighorn Fight and wore a magnificent war bonnet as a distinctive sign of his combat accomplishments. It was said that he was the owner of a very powerful protector in the form of a necklace. This charm consisted of strands of twisted buffalo hair which supported a small, flat, round stone. Affixed to it was a little bundle containing the dried heart of the swift hawk, and which had two of its feathers tied to it. This protected him in battle, and on more than one occasion he was merely scratched by a bullet. In a fight with the Crow Indians on the Big Horn River, Crazy Head was nicked by a bullet in the palm of his hand, in his leg, and in the body. He was knocked off his pony and was then counted coup on by the Crows who beat and kicked him around the head. Yet from all these wounds, Crazy Head was laid up only one day, after which he was totally recovered. Such was the power of his spiritual protector. Crazy Head had a brother named Sun Road and a sister named Corn Woman, the latter having married the well-known Cheyenne, Brave Wolf. See Llewellyn and Hoebel, *The Cheyenne Way*, 24-25; Grinnell, *The Cheyenne Indians*, Vol. II, 123-24; Marquis, *Wooden Leg*, 14, 211, 244.

night the warrior societies held dances and the chiefs agreed on a plan of battle. The warriors prepared ritually (Sioux). When the Indians knew that soldiers were coming, the three Cheyenne soldier societies—Crazy Dogs (60 members), Elks (60 members) and Foxes (60 members), each led by eight leaders—began taking turns watching the soldiers.

Since much honor would come to those who fought the soldiers first, a group of forty or fifty warriors (Wolf Tooth among them) left camp and rode past the members of the warrior societies for a distance of four or five miles east of the battlefield. They were halted by two Indian scouts sent to recall them with the news that the soldiers were already getting in position to attack the village from the southeast. The Crazy Dogs had held a "suicide" meeting the night before.[5]

Six Cheyennes were killed in the battle: Lame White Man (an Old Man Chief, and the eldest to die), Noisy Walking, Long Roach (killed east of Custer Ridge, near I and F Companies), Scabby (died in his lodge and was buried at the mouth of Prairie Dog Creek, in the rimrocks on what is [now] known as the Nash place). Informant can not immediately recall the names of other Cheyennes killed.[6]

Monument: The Arickaree [sic] scout Little Soldier's name was really Little Brave. He was a brother of Bobtail Bull. The third brother was in the battle with the Cheyennes,

---

[4]According to the Minneconjou, White Bull, Custer was discovered as early as June 22. In addition, Owns Bobtail Horse and two other Lakota scouts saw Custer at the sundance ground along the Rosebud on June 24. Little Wolf's small band of Cheyennes also had seen Custer near Busby and followed him on June 25 to the camps on the Little Bighorn. See Hardorff, *Lakota Recollections*, 109, and also the Bull Hump and White Bird Interview given heretofore.

[5]The statement about the "suicide" meeting has reference to a ceremonial dance during which a number of young Cheyennes and Lakotas allegedly vowed to die on the battlefield in the next fight. See Stands in Timber and Liberty, *Cheyenne Memories*, 194.

as he had been a Cheyenne since he was a little boy, and he was a noted warrior.[7]

Custer came toward the village from the high ridges to the east. The Custer men tried to cross the river at a ford west of the present railroad tracks, on what is now the Willy Bends place.[8] Cheyennes hidden in the brush on the south side of the ford drove the soldiers back and killed a couple of them in the brush by the river. Then the Custer men retreated to the flats below where the superintendent's house is now located. They waited there for about half an hour, while Indians assembled in the vicinity and fired on the soldiers from the ridges north of the flats. (Six empty 45/70 cases were found there subsequent to this interview, in a place where the cartridges could not have been fired at targets anywhere but on the flats mentioned.)

Stands in Timber said that the Indians wondered why the soldiers did not move south to rejoin the others, and that if Custer's men had not delayed so long, they could have gotten

---

[6]Actually seven Cheyennes were slain: Roman Nose, Limber Bones, Noisy Walking, Lame White Man, Cut Belly, Little Whirlwind, and Black Bear. Stands in Timber is incorrect about Long Roach who was not a Custer Battle casualty. However, he may have mistaken Long Roach with the latter's son, Roman Nose, who was slain during Reno's retreat from the valley floor. Scabby was a casualty of the Rosebud Fight. He was mortally wounded on present Kolmar Creek and died at the mouth of Prairie Dog Creek about June 20. See Hardorff, *Hokahey! A Good Day to Die!*, and also Stands in Timber and Liberty, *Cheyenne Memories*, 186–87. It should be kept in mind that Stands in Timber was past seventy at the time of this interview, and that he did not have the benefit of any notes. These memory errors were corrected by him in his publication.

[7]The name of this third brother was Plenty Crows who was captured at an early age and raised by the Cheyennes. Stands in Timber and Liberty, *Cheyenne Memories*, 209.

[8]According to Stands in Timber's description, this ford would have been about a mile south of the present junction of U.S. Highway 87 and U.S. Highway 212. This location would be on the west side of the present railroad tracks, which run parallel with and a hundred yards west of U.S. Highway 87. However, a map published in *Cheyenne Memories*, p. 196, contradicts Stands in Timber's statement because it clearly shows that Custer's force did not cross the present highway at all, but in fact shows that it remained well to the east of it.

back to the other soldiers. But by the time some of them (Gray Horse [Company]) did move toward the big ravine on the battlefield (E Co. Ravine) it was too late and the Indians were all around them in large numbers. When the Gray Horse Soldiers moved south, they were confronted by a large number of Indians in and near the big Ravine. Indians coming from the north and from the south forced the Gray Horse Soldiers in the big ravine.[9]

One soldier rode away from the rest (during the fight along the ridge) and went east. Low Dog and Little Son [Sun] chased him. Low Dog dismounted and, taking careful aim, shot the soldier from his horse as he topped the second ridge east of the Battlefield fence line.[10]

Lame White Man (killed near the top of Custer Ridge, on west slope, in about the center of the ridge) was not wearing his formal war clothes in the fight. According to Wolf Tooth and Tall Bull, he had just come from a sweat lodge, [and had] wrapped a blanket around his lower body and [had] taken his gun and ammunition with him. His hair was not braided, but loose. When found, a small scalp had been taken from his head.[11]

The first fighting in the Battlefield vicinity was at the ford on the west side of the valley. Lame White Man and most of the Cheyennes crossed here after the troops were driven back. All the soldiers, except the Gray Horse Soldiers, retreated afoot up the slope of Custer Ridge, driving the Indians east of the ridge. The soldiers in the ravine (Co. I and

---

[9]The Big Ravine mentioned is probably the present Deep Ravine.

[10]Low Dog was an Oglala Lakota who had Cheyenne relations. After the Custer Battle he sought sanctuary in Canada where he joined Sitting Bull's Hunkpapas. Upon his surrender in 1880, Low Dog settled among the Minneconjous along Cherry Creek on the Cheyenne River Agency, where he died about 1910. Note that Stands in Timber tells about the shooting of the white man in *Cheyenne Memories*, pp. 207-08, and identified the kill site as being "halfway to the head of Medicine Tail [Coulee]."

Co. F) had charged the Indians from near the river, but were outflanked by hostiles from the north and some from the south. These men were quickly surrounded, though they fought hard and moved in a southerly direction to the last.[12] A Ute (raised as a Cheyenne) named Yellow Nose found a soldier flag in the sagebrush along Custer Ridge. He wrapped it around his body as a prize. The horses of the Gray Horse Soldiers were frightened away by the Indians coming up the big ravine on the Battlefield. The [Lt. James] Calhoun soldiers were facing west at the last, and were the last ones to be killed.

Beginning of the battle: A band of forty or fifty warriors, returning to the village, met the Custer soldiers on a high ridge east of the battlefield. (As pointed out by Stands in Timber, this would be above and east of the Nye-Cartwright Ridge area. Shells have subsequently been found there, but more fieldwork is needed to prove or disprove this account of the fighting in this location.) After the first fighting, the soldiers came down in two lines to the Nye-Cartwright Ridge area.[13] The Gray Horse Soldiers acted as rear guard for about half an hour to hold off the Indians attacking from the south; then they followed the other soldiers along Nye-Cartwright

---

[11]The scalp was removed by the Minneconjou, Little Crow, a brother of Chief Hump, who mistook the Cheyenne for an Arikara Indian. The absence of war insignia and painting may have contributed to this misidentification. It should also be noted that among the Lakotas the practice of wearing one's hair loose in combat signified that the wearer was prepared to fight to the death. See Hardorff, *Lakota Recollections*, 121; and also James R. Walker, *Lakota Belief and Ritual* (Lincoln, 1980), 273.

[12]This combat scenario suggests that Custer's troops fell back from the river toward Custer Ridge, along which they then retreated southward to Calhoun Hill which thus became the actual location of the "Last Stand." Stands in Timber's statement is overwhelmingly contradicted by both Cheyenne and Lakota informants who stated categorically that the last stand was made at Custer Hill, and that the survivors from Calhoun Hill attempted to withdraw to this location. See, for example, the Camp Interviews in Hardorff, *Lakota Recollections*.

Ridge and onto Custer Battlefield. They all went along Custer Ridge, [and] then turned east [west?] to try and cross the river. Repulsed at the river, the soldiers then halted on the flats below the superintendent's house and below cemetery.

(Note: The battle proper began below and west of the cemetery [and then] moved to Custer Ridge. The troops were moving in a generally southerly or southeasterly direction as seen from a Cheyenne viewpoint.)

The Reno-Benteen Phase: The Reno soldiers moved north to where the Custer soldiers were killed. (According to this informant, the move came after the Custer men were dead, or at least defeated.) The Indians then went up the ravines east of Weir Point, and seeing them, the soldiers retreated again. The troops seemed to sense an ambush, as the hostiles were just waiting for them to advance a little farther before falling on them from the flank.

On the Reno field, some rocks east of the soldier position mark where a fifteen-year-old Sioux boy rode too close to the soldiers and was killed. His horse threw him, [and] then the boy was shot. The horse turned over in the air and then got up and ran away.[14] The rocks on the south end of Benteen Hill mark where Thunder Shield (a Sioux) was killed while trying to count coup on dead soldiers.[15]

Some Cheyennes fighting from Wooden Leg Hill were: Spotted Elk, Sleeping Rabbit, Sandstone, Big Ankles

---

[13]Situated about 1½ miles east of the Little Bighorn, on the south side of Deep Ravine, Nye-Cartwright Ridge was named after Lt. Col. Edward L. Nye and Ralph G. Cartwright who recovered numerous artifacts at this location. The initial artifact discovery was made by Joe Blummer who shared his findings with battlefield personnel and with Nye. For a discussion of the artifacts found at this location, see Richard G. Hardorff, *Markers*, 31-38.

[14]The name of this young Lakota was Breech Cloth who was killed near dusk on June 25, while charging in front of the breastworks on the east side of Reno Hill. See Hardorff, *Hokahey! A Good Day to Die!*, 86.

(Sioux), Wolf Tooth and Big Foot.[16] Big Ankles was a nephew of Lame Deer. He was killed in the lame Deer Fight. The Lame Deer Fight began because of him. While Lame Deer and Iron Star were talking to [Gen. Nelson A.] Miles, Big Ankles rode back and forth, and Miles asked that this be stopped. [When] a soldier tussled with Big Ankles over [the] possession of a gun, Big Ankles was accidentally shot, [and] then the fighting began. Stands in Timber lives at the site of the Lame Deer Fight.[17]

---

[15]Known to the Cheyennes as Thunder Shield, the Lakota name of this young Sans Arc was Long Road. It was said that he had grown despondent by the death of his older brother, a casualty of the Rosebud fight, and that thereafter Long Road did not want to live anymore. See Hardorff, *Hokahey! A Good Day to Die!*, 87–91

[16]At least two individuals among the Northern Cheyennes were named Sleeping Rabbit. One was a young man who surrendered with Two Moons' band at Ft. Keogh in 1877. The second individual was a well-known shaman who was known as far back as 1864 for his skill and success in stopping the flow of blood caused by wounds. He later became a civil leader. See Grinnell, *The Cheyenne Indians*, II, 158, and Llewellyn and Hoebel, *The Cheyenne Way*, 122.

[17]Lame Deer was a Minneconjou leader who was slain on May 17, 1877. After the battle, one of Lame Deer's sons, Flying By, returned to recover his father's body, but found it was decapitated, the trunk containing seventeen bullet wounds. A search for the missing head was made in vain, and Flying By assumed that it had been carried off by the troops as a trophy. See Hardorff, *Lakota Recollections*, 76. For an excellent review of this engagement, see Jerome A. Greene, "The Lame Deer Fight: Last Drama of the Sioux War of 1876-1877." *By Valor and Arms* (No. 3, 1978):11-21.

Bibliography and Index

Bibliography

ARCHIVAL SOURCES

Billings, Montana. Billings Public Library. Billings Clipping File.

Bloomington, Indiana. University of Indiana Library. Manuscripts Division. Robert S. Ellison Collection: Walter M. Camp Manuscripts.

Crow Agency, Montana. Custer Battlefield National Monument, National Park Service. Elizabeth B. Custer Collection.

Denver, Colorado. Denver Public Library. Western History Division. Robert S. Ellison Collection: Walter Mason Camp Papers.

Laramie, Wyoming. University of Wyoming Library. Western History Research Center. Special Collections: Agnes W. Spring Collection.

Los Angeles, California. Southwest Museum Library. Manuscripts Division: George B. Grinnell Collection.

New York. New York Public Library. Manuscript Division: Francis R. Hagner Collection.

Norman, Oklahoma. University of Oklahoma Library. Western History Collection: Walter S. Campbell Collection.

Provo, Utah. Brigham Young University Library. Manuscripts Division: Walter Mason Camp Manuscripts.

PRINTED SOURCES

Books

Berthrong, Donald J. *The Southern Cheyennes.* Norman: University of Oklahoma Press, 1963.

Bourke, John G. *On the Border with Crook.* New York: Charles Scribner's, 1891.

Boyes, William. *Surgeon's Diary.* Rockville: WJBM Associates, 1974.

Brown, Barron. *Comanche.* New York: Sol Lewis, 1973.

Brown, Mark H. and W.R. Felton. *The Frontier Years: L.A. Huffman, Photographer of the Plains.* New York: Henry Holt, 1955.

Burdick, Usher L. *David F. Barry's Notes on the Custer Battle.* Baltimore: Wirth Brothers, 1949.

Carroll, John M. *The Gibson-Edgerly Narratives.* Bryan, TX: privately printed, nd.

_____. *A Seventh Cavalry Scrapbook, #10.* Bryan: privately printed, 1979.

_____. *The Arrest and Killing of Sitting Bull: A Documentary.* Glendale: Arthur H. Clark Co., 1987.

Catlin, George. *Letters and Notes on the Manners, Customs, and Conditions of the North American Indians.* 2 vols. New York: Dover Publications, 1973.

Chandler, Melbourne C. *Of Garry Owen in Glory: The History of the Seventh United States Cavalry Regiment.* Annandale: privately printed, 1960.

Clark, Robert A., ed. *The Killing of Chief Crazy Horse.* Glendale: Arthur H. Clark Co., 1976.

Crawford, Lewis F. *Rekindling Camp Fires: The Exploits of Ben Arnold.* Bismarck: Capitol Book Co., 1926.

Curtis, Edward S. *The North American Indians, III.* Cambridge: The University Press, 1908.

Custer, George A. *My Life on the Plains.* Lincoln: University of Nebraska Press, 1966.

DeBarthe, Joe. *Life and Adventures of Frank Grouard.* Norman: University of Oklahoma Press, 1958.

DeMallie, Raymond J., ed. *The Sixth Grandfather: Black Elk's Teachings Given to John G. Neihardt.* Lincoln: University of Nebraska Press, 1984.

DeWall, Rob. *The Saga of Sitting Bull's Bones.* Crazy Horse: Korczak's Heritage, 1984.

Dixon, Joseph K. *The Vanishing Race.* New York: Bonanza Books, 1975.

du Mont, John S. *Custer Battle Guns.* Ft. Collins: Old Army Press, 1974.

Finerty, John F. *War-path and Bivouac, or, the Conquest of the Sioux.* Norman: University of Oklahoma Press, 1961.

Fox, Richard Allan, Jr. *Archaeology, History, and Custer's Last Battle.* Norman: Univ. of Okla. Press, 1993.

Gilbert, Hila. *"Big Bat" Pourier.* Sheridan: The Mills Company, 1968.

Graham, W.A. *The Custer Myth: A Source Book of Custeriana.* New York: Bonanza Books, 1953.

_____. *Abstract of the Official Record of the Reno Court of Inquiry.* Harrisburg: Stackpole, 1954.

Gray, John S. *Centennial Campaign: The Sioux War of 1876.* Ft. Collins: Old Army Press, 1976.

Grinnell, George Bird. *The Fighting Cheyennes.* Norman: University of Oklahoma Press, 1956.

_____. *By Cheyenne Campfires.* Lincoln: University of Nebraska Press, 1971.

_____. *The Cheyenne Indians.* 2 vols. Lincoln: University of Nebraska Press, 1972.

Hafen, LeRoy R. and Francis Marion Young. *Fort Laramie and the Pageant of the West, 1834-1890.* Lincoln: University of Nebraska Press, 1984.

Hammer, Kenneth. *Men with Custer.* Ft. Collins: Old Army Press, 1972.

_____., ed. *Custer in '76: Walter Camp's Notes on the Custer Fight.* Provo: Brigham Young University Press, 1976.

Hanson, Joseph Mills. *The Conquest of the Missouri.* New York: Murray Hill Books, 1946.

Hardorff, Richard G. *The Oglala Lakota Crazy Horse: A Preliminary Genealogical Study and an Annotated Listing of Primary Sources.* Mattituck: J.M. Carroll Company, 1985.

_____. *Markers, Artifacts and Indian Testimony: Preliminary Findings on the Custer Battle.* Short Hills: Don Horn Publications, 1985.

_____. *The Custer Battle Casualties: Burials, Exhumations and Reinterments.* El Segundo: Upton and Sons, Publishers, 1989.

_____. *Lakota Recollections of the Custer Fight: New Sources of Indian-Military History.* Spokane: Arthur H. Clark Co., 1991.

_____. *Hokahey! A Good Day to Die! The Indian Casualties of the Custer Fight.* Spokane: Arthur H. Clark Co., 1993.

Hyde, George E. *Red Cloud's Folk: A History of the Oglala Sioux Indians.* Norman: University of Oklahoma Press, 1937.

_____. *Life of George Bent.* Norman: University of Oklahoma Press, 1968.

Langellier, J., K. Cox, and B.C. Pohanka, eds. *Myles Keogh: The Life and Legend of an Irish Dragoon in the Seventh Cavalry.* El Segundo, CA: Upton and Sons, 1991.

Lawrence, Elizabeth. *His Very Silence Speaks: Comanche, The Horse Who Survived Custer's Last Stand.* Detroit: Wayne State University Press, 1989.

Libby, Orin G., ed. *The Arikara Narrative of the Campaign Against the Hostile Dakotas, June 1876.* New York: Sol Lewis, 1973.

Linderman, Frank. *Pretty-Shield.* Lincoln: University of Nebraska Press, 1972.

Llewellyn, K.N. and E.A. Hoebel. *The Cheyenne Way: Conflict and Case Law in Primitive Jurisprudence.* Norman: University of Oklahoma Press, 1941.

Magnussen, Daniel O. *Peter Thompson's Narrative of the Little Bighorn Campaign, 1876.* Glendale: Arthur H. Clark Co., 1974.

Mangum, Neil C. *The Battle of the Rosebud.* El Segundo: Upton and Sons, Publishers, 1987.

Marquis, Thomas B. *Wooden Leg.* Lincoln: University of Nebraska Press, 1962.

_____. *Custer on the Little Bighorn.* Lodi: End-Kian Publishing, 1971.

_____. *Cheyennes and Sioux.* Stockton: University of Pacific Press, 1973.

_____. *Keep the Last Bullet for Yourself.* New York: Two Continents Publishing Co., 1976.

McClernand, Edward J. *With the Indian and the Buffalo in Montana, 1870-1878.* Glendale: Arthur H. Clark Co., 1969.

McCracken, Harold. *Frederick Remington's Own West.* New York: Promontory Press, 1960.

McLaughlin, James. *My Friend the Indian.* Seattle: Superior Publishing, 1970.

Miles, Nelson A. *Personal Recollections and Observations of General Nelson A. Miles.* New York: Werner Co., 1897.

Milligan, Edward A. *High Noon on the Greasy Grass*. Bottineau: Bottineau Courant, 1972.

Monaghan, Jay. *Custer: Life of General George Custer*. Lincoln: University of Nebraska Press, 1971.

Olson. James C. *Red Cloud and the Sioux Problem*. Lincoln: University of Nebraska Press, 1965.

Powell, Peter J. and Michael P. Malone. *Montana, Past and Present*. Los Angeles: University of California Press, 1986.

Sandoz, Mari. *Cheyenne Autumn*. New York: McGraw Hill, 1953.

_____. *Crazy Horse: The Strange Man of the Oglalas*. Lincoln: University of Nebraska Press, 1961.

Schmitt, Martin F. *General George Crook: His Autobiography*. Norman: University of Oklahoma Press, 1946.

Scott, Douglass D. and Richard A. Fox, Jr. *Archaeological Insights into the Custer Battle*. Norman: University of Oklahoma Press, 1987.

_____, et al. *Archaeological Perspectives on the Battle of the Little Bighorn*. Norman: University of Oklahoma Press, 1989.

Standing Bear, Luther. *My People the Sioux*. Lincoln: University of Nebraska Press, 1975.

Stands in Timber, John and Margot Liberty. *Cheyenne Memories*. Lincoln: University of Nebraska Press, 1972.

Stewart, Edgar I. *Custer's Luck*. Norman: University of Oklahoma Press, 1955.

Utley, Robert M., intro. *The Reno Court of Inquiry: The Chicago Times Account*. Ft. Collins: Old Army Press, 1972.

Vaughn, J.W. *With Crook on the Rosebud*. Harrisburg: Stackpole, 1956.

_____. *The Reynolds Campaign on Powder River*. Norman: University of Oklahoma Press, 1961.

_____. *Indian Fights*. Norman: University of Oklahoma Press, 1966.

Vestal, Stanley. *Sitting Bull, Champion of the Sioux*. Boston: Houghton Mifflin, 1932.

_____. *Warpath: The True Story of the Fighting Sioux: Told in a Biography of Chief White Bull*. Boston: Houghton Mifflin, 1934.

_____. *Warpath and Council Fire*. New York: Random House, 1948.

Wagner, Glendolin D. *Old Neutriment*. New York: Sol Lewis, 1973.

Articles

Eastman, Charles H. "Rain-in-the-Face." *The Outlook* (October 27, 1906).

Greene, Jerome A. "Evidence and the Custer Enigma: A Reconstruction of Indian-Military History." *The Westerners Trail Guide* (Kansas City) (March-June, 1973).

Marshall, Robert A. How Many Indians Were There? *Research Review* (Little Big Horn Associates) (June, 1977).

Rickey, Jr., Don. "Myth to Monument: The Establishment of Custer Battlefield National Monument." *Journal of the West* (April, 1968).

Roberts, Gary L. "The Shame of Little Wolf." *Montana, The Magazine of Western History* (Summer, 1978).

Newspapers

Billings (Montana) *Daily Gazette,* 1911
Billings Gazette, 1926, 1927, 1961
Bismarck (North Dakota) *Tribune,* 1877
Hardin (Montana) *Tribune,* 1923
St. Paul Pioneer Press, 1886

Index